WHAT WE BELIEVE:

AN EXPOSITION OF THE APOSTLES' CREED

WHAT WE BELIEVE:

AN EXPOSITION OF THE APOSTLES' CREED

Cornelis P. Venema

Reformed Fellowship
4855 Star Street S.E.
Grand Rapids, Michigan 49546
U.S.A.

Reformed Fellowship Inc.
2930 Chicago Drive, S.W.
Grandville, MI 49418-1176
USA

© Reformed Fellowship, Inc., 1996
ISBN 0-9653981-1-0

TABLE OF CONTENTS

PREFACE

It has become fashionable in recent years to decry the absence of discernment and biblical understanding on the part of many Christian believers in North America. Well-known authors like Mark Noll and David Wells have written books with titles like, *The Scandal of the Evangelical Mind*, *No Place for Truth*, and *God in the Wasteland*.

Often missing from the diagnosis of this absence of biblical and doctrinal understanding among believers today is the neglect of the church's creeds and confessions. In the history of the Christian church, believers were traditionally taught the Scriptures *in terms of the summaries provided in the creeds or the confessions.* The use of catechisms, for example, to teach the truth of the Word of God has been an indispensable component of the teaching ministry of the church.

This study of the Apostles' Creed is offered, accordingly, to encourage a renewed appreciation for and use of the creeds and confessions in the church's educational ministry. Next to the study of the Word of God in Scripture, no more profitable exercise can be imagined than the study of the great creeds and confessions of the Christian church. The Apostles' Creed is a likely place to begin such a study, since it is the most universal and basic of all the creeds and confessions.

The chapters of this study were originally written for a column in *The Outlook*, a monthly periodical devoted to the propagation and defense of the historic Reformed faith. Recommended readings and questions for discussion have been added with each chapter to enhance their value as a basis for study and reflection.

Scripture references throughout have been taken from the New American Standard Version of the Bible. Frequently, I have referred to the Heidelberg Catechism's explanation of articles in the Apostles' Creed. These Catechism references are taken from the English translation in the 1979 edition of the *Ecumenical Creeds and Confessions*, published by the Board of Publications of the Christian Reformed Church.

CHAPTER ONE

INTRODUCING THE APOSTLES' CREED

"If you confess with your mouth Jesus as Lord, and believe in your heart that God raised Him from the dead, you shall be saved; for with the heart man believes, resulting in righteousness, and with the mouth he confesses, resulting in salvation." Romans 10:9-10

Ours is an age which prizes as a virtue the attitude of open-mindedness or broad-mindedness. We praise the person who is willing to consider a variety of viewpoints, who does not too hastily commit himself to one over the other, and who resists being critical of the opinions of others. Conversely, we are suspicious of those who are confident about what they believe and confess to be true. We fear that such people may be arrogant and intolerant of the opinions of others.

Furthermore, many even doubt whether there is such a thing as *the truth* which may be known and confessed. Alan Bloom, in his best-selling book, *The Closing of the American Mind,*[1] has described the grip which this relativism has upon American culture and its students. When people are convinced that there is no truth to be known, their minds become closed and the pursuit after truth appears to them to be futile. Who knows what is true or false? How do we come to know what is true? What are we

---

[1]New York, NY: Simon and Schuster, 1987.

authorized to believe? These questions are raised but they go begging for answers. And the person who thinks he can answer them is suspected of being proudly presumptuous and narrow-minded.

Biblical Christians — are there any other kind? — must reckon with this feature of the world in which we live. For it has influenced all of us deeply, whether we are prepared to admit it or not. Our hesitancy to state what we believe and confess to be the truth is often born out of an unrecognized accommodation to this relativistic spirit. Or, it is born out of a lack of confidence that we have a *sure Word* from God in the Scriptures on the basis of which we can know and confess the truth.

In contrast to the pervasive relativism of our culture, this exposition of the Apostles' Creed will proceed from the settled confidence that we do have a sure Word of God in Scripture. We will begin with that certainty of faith of which the Heidelberg Catechism, one of the most sparkling confessions to emerge during the Protestant Reformation, speaks, when it defines faith in part as "a knowledge and conviction that everything God reveals in His Word is true...."[2] We will operate from the conviction that what we believe is to be determined by a faithful listening to the Word of God in the Scriptures.

The role of confession in the life of a Christian

Before providing a brief introduction to the Apostles' Creed, however, I would like to begin by noting how, in the Scriptures, to be a Christian is to be someone who confesses the truth. Confessing the truth lies very close to the heart of what it means to be a Christian.

It is evident in the Scriptures themselves that a believer is by definition one who cannot escape the obligation to confess what he believes on the basis of the revelation of God's truth in His

---

[2]Quoted from the English translation in *Ecumenical Creeds and Reformed Confessions* (Grand Rapids, MI: Board of Publications of the Christian Reformed Church, 1979), p. 13. Throughout this study, the quotations from the creeds and confessions will be taken from this volume, unless otherwise noted.

Word. Though we cannot consider all the relevant passages here, a few should be sufficient to confirm this fact.

In his first letter to Timothy, the apostle Paul concludes his instruction with the exhortation, "Fight the good fight of faith; take hold of the eternal life to which you were called, and you made the good confession in the presence of many witnesses" (1 Tim. 6:12). Timothy is here exhorted to steadfastness in the good confession which he once made in the presence of many witnesses. This good confession, in which Timothy apparently abandoned the way of unbelief and entered upon the course of faith, though it involves him in a struggle and a fight, will issue in eternal life. Paul also notes that Timothy in making this good confession was following the pattern of Christ who Himself made a good confession before Pontius Pilate (v. 13). Though we are not told what the content of this confession was, it is important to note that it was a decisive and necessary expression of Timothy's faith and commitment to Jesus Christ. No one who bears the name Christian can neglect likewise to make such a good confession in the presence of witnesses.

Similarly, in Romans 10:8-10, the apostle Paul speaks of the necessity of publicly confessing one's faith in response to the Word of God:

> The Word is near you, in your mouth and in your heart — that is, the word of faith which we are preaching, that if you confess with your mouth Jesus as Lord, and believe in your heart that God raised Him from the dead, you shall be saved; for with the heart man believes, resulting in righteousness, and with the mouth he confesses, resulting in salvation.

Here a close relationship is posited between the Word which is heard and believed, and the open confession of faith in what that Word teaches concerning Jesus as Lord and His resurrection from the dead. There is a kind of unbroken chain linking together Word, faith and confession. The Word of the gospel, where it is believed, is always openly confessed and this confession brings salvation!

Consequently, we find frequently in the Scriptures that those who believe the Word give expression to what they believe in the form of a confession of faith. Their confession is focused upon the person and work of Jesus Christ. It is a public declaration of their subscription to the truth of the Word concerning Him. And it is of decisive consequence for their salvation. This is evident, for example, in John 4:41,42, where we read, "And many more believed because of His word; and they were saying to the woman, 'It is no longer because of what you said that we believe, for we have heard for ourselves and know that this One is indeed the Savior of the world." In Matthew 10:32,33, Christ promises that He will confess before the Father the names of those who confess Him before men: "Everyone therefore who shall confess Me before men, I will also confess him before My Father who is in heaven. But whoever shall deny Me before men, I will also deny him before My Father who is in heaven." The same decisiveness and importance of this confession is underscored in John 6:68-69, where we find Simon Peter speaking on behalf of the disciples, "Lord, to whom shall we go? You have words of eternal life. And we have believed and have come to know that You are the Holy One of God."

When a good and true confession is made upon the basis of the Word of God, it is also said to be the fruit of the revelation of the Father and the operation of the Spirit through the Word. Thus, the apostle Paul can identify the confession, "Jesus is Lord," with a "speaking by the Holy Spirit," that is, a speaking which is the fruit of the Spirit's testimony through the Word (1 Cor. 12:3). Or, when Christ posed the decisive question to his disciples, "[B]ut who do you say that I am?," Peter responded with the confession, "Thou art the Christ, the Son of the living God" (Matt. 16:15-16). What is striking at this point is how Christ identifies the source of this confession, upon which He will build His church, with the Father who has revealed it from heaven. No one who is a Christian can escape this call to confess his faith in response to the Word of God.

It is remarkable how different this is from the spirit of our age! As believers we must be prepared and unashamed to make our confession of faith before the world, however unpopular and unwelcome that may be in a world committed to only one absolute — that there are no absolutes! We must not hesitate in maintaining that this belongs to the essence of our faith — that we hold for true what God reveals in His Word and openly confess this truth before others.

Creeds and confessions

Given the prominence and necessity of making public confession of what we believe, it is not surprising that the history of the church has been characterized by the writing of formal creeds and confessions, of which the Apostles' Creed is the best known. Even though among some evangelical Christians there has been a tendency to disparage creeds and confessions — consider the slogan, "no creed but Christ" — the formulation of what Christians believe in the form of a credal or confessional statement has been an integral part of the witness and ministry of the church through the centuries.

For this reason, it is important to define carefully what we mean by a "creed" or a "confession." What is a creed? What is a confession?

We can obtain a partial answer to these questions by simply noting the meaning of these terms. The term, "creed," comes from a Latin root and derives historically from the opening words of many of the ancient creeds of the church, particularly the Apostles' and Nicene Creeds. These words, "I believe," or "credo," indicate that the following affirmations are a summary of what the individual Christian believes or is convinced of from the Scriptures. On the other hand, the term, "confession," literally means "to say with," that is, to give expression to what Christians believe in common. A confession is a statement of faith, of what the Christian church believes, which believers make in common with other believers. You might say that a confession is a "saying the same thing with one heart and voice." Creeds and confessions, accordingly, are summaries of what Christians believe and wish publicly to affirm as the content of their faith.

But what difference, if any, is there between a "creed" and a "confession"? Though it is unwise to press too much the difference between creed and confession, some observations are permissible. The term "creed" has historically been reserved to describe the three so-called "ecumenical" creeds, the Apostles' Creed, the Nicene Creed, and the Athanasian Creed. What distinguishes these creeds from the confessions is their relative brevity. They are short, compact statements or summaries of Christian conviction, unlike the confessions which are often much more extensive and detailed. They are also ordinarily written in the first person singular ("I believe") form, and have originated in or been fashioned for appropriate liturgical use. As we shall see, for example, with the Apostles' Creed, the origin of the creed is often closely linked with the public worship and service of the Christian church and, therefore, many believers will readily recognize the creeds from their recitation in the worship services. They are "ecumenical" because they are the common confession of the Christian church worldwide.

The confessions of the churches have a somewhat different character from that of the creeds. Though, like the creed, a formal statement of faith, the confessions are often written in a more objective and less personal manner. They do not necessarily have the form of the "I believe."[3] The confessions also are more elaborate statements of the faith of the Christian churches that embrace them. Many of these confessions, especially those that were written in the time of the Protestant Reformation in the sixteenth century, re-affirm the early creeds and confessions of the church and then go on to indicate articles of doctrine or faith that distinguish those who make this confession from others who may disagree with it. Thus, the confessions, though they often serve as "forms of unity" to join in faith those who acknowledge them as their own, frequently serve to *distinguish* the faith of one congregation or fellowship of congregations from others. There are, in this respect, Lutheran, Reformed, Baptist, Methodist and

---

[3]Clearly, this is a relative point of difference, since many of the confessions of the churches are actually catechisms, statements of Christian conviction given in question and answer format, which often employ throughout the first person singular.

other kinds of confessions, each of which serves to identify the distinctive convictions of these respective churches.[4]

Sometimes these creeds and confessions are also termed "symbols." This language is used to underscore the public, corporate nature of the creed and confession. They are "symbols" or "badges" of Christian confession that serve to identify the Christian church and those who belong to it in terms of their distinctive commitments and convictions. They are symbols of the uniqueness of the Christian faith and the opposition that obtains between those who identify with that faith and those who do not.

The purposes of creeds and confessions

Despite the indispensable role of confession in the life of the believer, and despite the long history of the writing of creeds and confessions in Christian tradition, there remain those who object to creeds and confessions. We have already acknowledged one such objection — that, because "no one has a corner on the truth," creeds and confessions illegitimately claim to be affirmations of *the* truth. But there are additional objections.

One objection is that we should have "no creed but Christ." What matters is the Christian's personal relationship to Jesus Christ, not whether he subscribes to a particular creed or confession. The problem with this objection is that it is self-defeating. It suffers from the fallacy of believing you can have a relationship with, or be committed to, Jesus Christ without any knowledge of the truth concerning Him as that is revealed through the gospel

---

[4]Cf. Philip Schaff in his important study, *Creeds of Christendom*, vol. 1, sixth ed. (New York, NY: Harper & Row, 1931), pp. 9-11, where he distinguishes four kinds of creeds and confessions: the ecumenical symbols of the ancient church; the symbols of the Greek or Oriental churches; the symbols of the Roman Catholic Church, from the Council of Trent onward; and the symbols of the evangelical, Protestant churches. Klaas Runia, in his *I Believe in God: Current Questions and the Creeds* (Chicago, IL: Intervarsity, 1963), speaks of the creeds as "marks of unity" and the confessions as "marks of disunity." The problem with this distinction is that, though it properly shows how the confessions often serve to distinguish as much as they unite believers, it does not adequately acknowledge that the confessions *ought* to unite believers in the truth. A Reformed believer, for example, ought to be so convinced of his confession that he desires that all other believers join in making the same confession.

recorded in the Old and New Testament Scriptures. It is mean-
ingless to speak of "Jesus Christ," *unless you are prepared to
identify who He is, why He is your Savior and Lord, and the like.*
But to do so requires either subscribing to some creed or confession regarding Him, or subscribing to the common creed or
confession of the Christian churches. The wiser policy in this
circumstance, of course, would be to join other believers in
making a common confession on the basis of the Bible's teaching.

Another objection, which initially has more plausibility, says
that "the Bible alone" (*sola Scriptura*) is sufficient. Some who
offer this objection would add that the creed or confession
inevitably endangers the authority and sufficiency of the Bible,
since it expresses in human, non-inspired words what the Bible
expresses in divine or God-given words. Since we cannot improve
upon the gospel record in the Bible, why should we be distracted
by creeds and confessions? The truth of this objection lies in its
recognition that *the creed or confession is always subordinate in its
authority to the Bible.* The creed or confession can only echo the
teaching of Scripture. However, that is precisely the reason the
creed or confession must have its place. Believers, whether as
individuals or in concert with other believers, are obligated to
declare what they have heard and believe on the basis of the
Bible. That's why the creed or confession has been called a
"repetition of Sacred Scripture" (*repetitio Sacrae Scripturae*). In
the creed or confession, believers offer their response, confessing
as truth what they have heard in the Word of God.

It is not difficult to add to these objections still others. It is
frequently alleged, for example, that the creed or confession
betrays "Christian liberty" and freedom of individual conscience.
Or it is objected that the creed or confession can prove divisive.
Working together as believers on a variety of projects is a policy
that is unifying. However, whenever the creed or confession
comes into play, divisions soon develop or become more pronounced. In more recent times, it is even argued that the creed
or confession is a hindrance to the work of evangelism. If new
believers are required to learn and know the creed or confession,

this will throw up a barrier to their incorporation into the fellowship of the church.

Rather than multiplying these objections or attempting to continue to answer each one individually, the best way to address them all is to recall the various purposes served by the creeds and confession. In this way, it will be evident why the creeds and confessions are always indispensable to the life and mission of the churches of Jesus Christ.

First, consistent with what we have already said about the relation of Word, faith and confession, the creeds and confessions are fundamentally summaries, of varying length and scope, of Scriptural teaching. They have a *declarative* purpose. These confessions identify the church and those who are members of the church. They belong to the life of the church as a confessing and confessional community. It is for this reason that the church's confessions have been termed her "standards," "symbols," or even "rules of faith" (*regula fidei*). By means of these common or shared confessions, the church and her members declare publicly and openly, on the basis of the Word of God, what they believe and are convinced of.

Second, the creeds and confessions are always a safeguard against heresy or that which may not be believed because it contradicts the teaching of the Word of God. In this respect, the creeds and confessions serve a *defensive* or *apologetic* purpose. Interestingly, most of the historic creeds and confessions of the church have arisen in a circumstance of conflict between faith and unbelief, between the truth and the lie. They affirm in order to deny. When the church, for example, formulated her confession concerning the person of Jesus Christ, she did so in conscious opposition to heresies which denied His eternal Sonship and deity.

Third, the creeds and confessions are an indispensable instrument for the instruction of those who are admitted into the fellowship of the church through profession of faith. This is the *educational* purpose of the creed. From the earliest period of the church's history, the creed served as a basic tool for catechesis, for the instruction of the faithful in the teaching of Scripture with a view to admission into the church's membership. Many of the creeds were first formulated for this very purpose or were incorporated into catechisms and used to instruct in the teachings of the Word of God. An obvious example of this is the incorporation of the Apostles' Creed into many historic catechisms, including the Heidelberg Catechism's exposition of the content of the faith.

Fourth, the creeds and confessions are the "form" of the church's unity. To "confess" is to "say together with" others what one believes. The creeds and confessions serve a *unitive* purpose. This is the essential basis of the church's unity — her common confession of what she believes. Rather than serving to divide and to splinter the church, the creed serves to join together those who express what they believe in the words of the creed. It is for this reason that we speak of various "ecumenical" creeds which express the shared and common faith of the churches of Jesus Christ throughout the world. And it is for this reason that we speak of the Reformed confessions as the "forms of unity" which serve to unite all Reformed churches in their common understanding of the Word of God.

Fifth, the creeds and confessions are integral to the church's worship. This is their *doxological* or *liturgical* purpose. Some of the earliest summaries of faith were used in conjunction with the baptism of new converts. They were also used on the occasion of the administration of the sacrament of the Lord's Supper, a sacrament which is given to nourish and strengthen the faith of those who are professing members of the church. Here the creeds serve to unite the church and her members in their public worship of God.

And *sixth*, the creeds and confessions often play an important role in directing the public preaching of the gospel and the ministry of those who are appointed to offices in the churches. The creeds and confessions, so far as they are held to be binding upon those who preach the gospel as ministers of the Word or care for the congregations as elders and deacons, have a *juridical* function. They insure the uniformity of teaching and preaching in the churches, and guard the churches against the intrusion of false teaching through unbiblical preaching and teaching.

Introducing the Apostles' Creed

Perhaps the best known of the creeds and confessions of the Christian church is the Apostles' Creed. As an introduction to our consideration of its affirmations in the following chapters, the history and background of this popular, ecumenical Creed needs to be considered.

Authored by the apostles?

As the name of this Creed suggests, there has been a long tradition of ascribing it to the apostles whom Christ appointed and commissioned to be His representatives in the first period of the Christian era.

The earliest witnesses to the tradition of ascribing apostolic authorship to this Creed date to the latter part of the fourth century A.D. First Ambrose and then more extensively Rufinus expressed the conviction that the articles of this Creed were written by the twelve apostles. In his exposition of the Creed written circa 404 A.D., Rufinus tells the following story of this Creed's origin.

> As they were therefore on the point of taking leave of each other, they [the apostles] first settled an agreed norm for their future preaching, so that they might not find themselves, widely separated as they would be, giving out different doctrines to the people they invited to believe in Christ. So they met together in one spot and, being filled with the Holy Spirit, compiled this brief token, as I have said, of their future preaching, each making the contribution he thought fit; and they decreed that it should be handed out as standard teaching to believers.[5]

This legend, greatly expanded and embellished through time, became a commonplace during the Middle Ages. Each of the

---

[5] As cited by J.N.D. Kelly, *Early Christian Creeds* (London: Longmans, Green & Co., 1950), p. 1.

twelve apostles was said to have contributed one of the articles of the Creed. J.N.D. Kelly notes that, in addition to the pictorial expression of this legend in prayer books and church windows, a church in Trier was supported by twelve columns decorated with representations of the apostles and the articles of the Creed attributed to them.[6]

It is not difficult to understand the significance of this legend regarding the writing of the Apostles' Creed. The apostles were the Christ-appointed witnesses of the resurrection of Jesus Christ (John 20:19-23). They were instrumental in laying the foundation of the New Testament church through their Spirit-authored testimony concerning the person and work of the Lord Jesus Christ (Eph. 2:20; John 16:7-15). If the Apostles' Creed were indeed the fruit of their combined labors, it would have a unique and unparalleled authority as a summary of the Christian faith. It would be not only a distillation of the Scripture's teaching regarding the gospel of Jesus Christ, but it would also have the sanction of apostolic authorship.

However, it was inevitable that this legend would be exposed and the fact that the Apostles' Creed did not enjoy direct apostolic authorship be acknowledged. In the Eastern Orthodox Church, the Apostles' Creed never did enjoy wide acceptance and its apostolic authorship was soon challenged. At the Council of Florence in 1438-45, the Eastern delegates challenged the genuineness of this Creed.[7] And soon afterward the Renaissance scholar, Lorenzo Valla, undermined the legend of its apostolic origins. John Calvin, during the period of the Reformation, also conceded that this Creed was not written by the apostles directly, though he acknowledged its authority as a faithful summary of the Bible's teaching.

---

[6]Kelly, *Early Christian Creeds*, p. 4.

[7]Due to the reluctance of the Eastern Orthodox Churches to recognize the Apostle's Creed, a reluctance in part born out of its schism with the Western churches, the Apostle's Creed is not in the strictest sense an "ecumenical" creed. In the Eastern Orthodox Churches, only those creeds formulated by the ecumenical councils that met before the schism between East and West in 1054 A.D. deserve to be termed and received as ecumenical.

I call it the Apostles' Creed without concerning myself in the least as to its authorship. With considerable agreement, the old writers certainly attribute it to the apostles in common, or to be a summary of teaching transmitted by their hands and collected in good faith, and thus worthy of that title. I have no doubt that at the very beginning of the church, in the apostolic age, it was received as a public confession by the consent of all — wherever it originated. It seems not to have been privately written by any one person, since as far aback as men can remember it was certainly held to be of sacred authority among all the godly. We consider to be beyond controversy the only point that ought to concern us: that the whole history of our faith is summed up in it succinctly and in definite order, and that it contains nothing that is not vouched for by genuine testimonies of Scripture. This being understood, it is pointless to trouble oneself or quarrel anyone over the author.[8]

These words of Calvin are wise and fitting. Though it is generally conceded today that the story of the apostles' involvement in the writing of this Creed was a convenient legend, this Creed remains without peer as a summary of the ecumenical faith of the Christian church. It may not be apostolic in the narrow sense of having the apostles as its authors. But it is apostolic in the best and most important sense of the term — in its summary of the teaching of the apostles, as this teaching is revealed to us in the Scriptures.

The origin and use of this creed

However, if the Apostles' Creed does not owe its origin to the hand of the twelve apostles, what accounts for its origin and use in the churches?

[8]*Institutes of the Christian Religion*, ed. by John T. McNeill, 2 vols. (Philadelphia, PA: Westminster, 1960), II.xvi.18.

Originally the Apostles' Creed was a brief formula used at baptism when the believer was received into the church. In the church at Rome, a brief forerunner of our Apostles' Creed was in use already in the year 150 A.D. It may have been employed as part of a three-fold interrogation based upon the Trinitarian form of institution of baptism in Matt. 28:19 ("Go therefore and make disciples of all the nations, baptizing them in the name of the Father and the Son and the Holy Spirit."). The believer who was baptized was asked to confess his faith in God the Father Almighty, Jesus Christ His Only-begotten Son, and the Holy Spirit.

This brief statement was expanded in time to its present or "received form" in which it is divided into three articles comprised of twelve affirmations. The various stages in this expansion are somewhat obscure. No one knows with any certainty exactly how the present form of this Creed, as it is used and confessed in the churches of the West, came to be fixed.[9] We do know, however, that this present form of the Creed was secured by the late sixth or early seventh century. After this period, with the assistance of Charlemagne who sought to enforce a policy of uniformity in doctrine and practice throughout the Western Christian church, the Creed became in its received form the most universal standard and summary of Christian teaching.

No creed is better known or more widely used in the churches of Jesus Christ to identify the faith of those who are incorporated through baptism into Christ and His church, to provide for the instruction of new confessors, or to provide a unifying confession of faith for worship and liturgy.

In the Apostles' Creed, therefore, we have an excellent standard with which to measure what we believe as Christians upon the basis of the Word of God.

---

[9]See Schaff, *The Creeds of Christendom*, vol. 1, pp. 45-55, for a history and comparative study of the various forms of the Apostle's Creed. In subsequent chapters, when we consider the various articles of the Apostle's Creed, there will be occasion to mention variations in the form of the Creed where they are of some importance.

Recommended reading:

Kelly, J.N.D. *Early Christian Creeds.* London: Longmans, Green & Co., 1950.

Runia, Klaas. *I Believe in God: Current Questions and the Creeds.* Chicago, IL: Intervarsity, 1963.

Schaff, Philip. *The Creeds of Christendom.* Vol. 1, sixth ed. New York, NY: Harper & Row, 1931.

Young, Frances. *The Making of the Creeds.* Philadelphia, PA: Trinity Press International, 1991.

Woolley, Paul. "What is a Creed For? Some Answers from History," in *Scripture and Confession*, ed. by John H. Skilton (Philadelphia, PA: Presbyterian & Reformed, 1973):95-124.

Questions for discussion

1. In this chapter, the following Scriptural texts are cited in respect to the place of confessing and confession in the Christian life: 1 Timothy 6:12-13; Romans 10:8-10; Matthew 10:32-33; and Matthew 16:15-16. Look up these texts and discuss their teaching about the role of confession in the life of a believer and the Christian church.

2. Define what is meant by "creed" or "confession." What are the similarities and differences between creeds and confessions? Illustrate these similarities and differences from creeds or confessions with which you are familiar.

3. Why are some of the creeds called "ecumenical"?

4. Philip Schaff has distinguished four kinds of creeds and confessions. Identify what kinds they are.

5. Many people today (some within as well as some outside of the church) strongly object to creeds and confessions. What are some of the more common objections to the creeds and confessions of the church? How would you answer these objections?

6. What are some of the primary purposes of the creeds?

7. How would you show that the creeds are useful, even necessary, to the evangelistic and missionary work of the church?

8. Describe the background and history of the Apostles' Creed.

CHAPTER TWO

"I BELIEVE IN GOD THE FATHER, ALMIGHTY, MAKER OF HEAVEN AND EARTH"

"Father the hour has come; glorify Thy Son, that the Son may glorify Thee. ... And this is eternal life, that they may know Thee, the only true God, and Jesus Christ whom Thou hast sent." John 17:1,3

The first article of the Apostles' Creed — "I believe in God the Father, Almighty, Maker of Heaven and Earth" — perfectly corresponds to the nature of the Creed itself. It could serve as a summary of the whole. This accounts for the immediate difficulty we face, when we come to consider its meaning — where do we begin and where do we end! For this article in short-hand form summarizes the whole of the Christian faith as a confession of faith in the true and the living God, Father, Son and Holy Spirit. It touches upon the doctrines of God, of creation, of providence, of the relation between God and His people, of Christ, of redemption. There is really no aspect of what we believe as Christians that could not be considered under the heading of this first article in the Creed.

In order to focus our consideration of this first article of the Creed, therefore, we will consider: first, what it affirms about who God is and how He is to be known; second, what it affirms about God as the Creator; and third, what implications this confession has for our life as believers.

17

The Triune God

In our introduction to the Apostles' Creed, we noted that it is structured in a Trinitarian way, following the pattern of the traditional baptismal words, "I baptize you into the name of the Father, the Son, and the Holy Spirit" (Matt. 28:20).

This is immediately evident in this first article. The God in whom the Christian places his trust and whom he claims to know through the revealed Word, is the "Father Almighty." This confession of God as the Almighty Father immediately reminds us that He is first of all the eternal Father of the only-begotten Son, who lives eternally with the Son in the communion of the Holy Spirit. Though the Apostles' Creed does not expressly speak of the Trinity, it is fundamentally a confession of faith in the Triune God, the one, true and living God who exists eternally as Father, Son and Holy Spirit, world without end.

Consequently, we must consider here the historic doctrine of the Trinity, since the Creed's confession of God as the Almighty Father does not only mean that He is our Father for Christ, His only-begotten Son's, sake, but also that He is the eternal Father of the only-begotten Son.

The doctrine of the Trinity teaches that while God is one, He exists in three Persons. The one true God is eternally Father, Son and Holy Spirit. These three Persons are not three individual persons in the sense in which we speak of persons. They are the three co-equal and co-essential members of the Trinity. There is within God Himself a threefold and essential relationship of the Father who eternally begets the Son, the Son who is eternally begotten of the Father, and the Holy Spirit who eternally proceeds from the Father and the Son. Though the Triune God dwells in light unapproachable and we can never comprehend Him fully (1 Tim. 6:16; John 1:18), the Christian confidently confesses that He is eternally as He has revealed Himself to us — Father, Son and Holy Spirit. As the Athanasian Creed, another of the early ecumenical creeds of the church, declares: "[I]n this Trinity none is afore, or after another; none is greater, or less than another. But the whole three persons are co-eternal, and co-equal.

So that in all things, as aforesaid, the Unity in Trinity and the Trinity in Unity is to be worshipped."[10]

One of the most common and tempting mistakes that is often made at this point is the attempt to find some analogy to the Trinity within the creation, in order to help us understand or comprehend our confession that there is one God who eternally exists in three Persons. Some, like Augustine, the great church father, have employed a "psychological" analogy, comparing the threeness of the Trinity to the difference, for example, between memory, understanding and will in one human mind. This analogy, however, tends to deny the real threeness of person between the Father, Son and Holy Spirit. Another analogy more commonly cited today is the "social" analogy, comparing the threeness of the Trinity to three individual persons who dwell in a state of perfect oneness of purpose and will. This analogy, however, tends to deny the real oneness of the three Persons and leads to tritheism or the doctrine of three "gods." The most appropriate approach for us to take here is simply to confess the unity in Trinity in the restrained form of the creeds, without seeking to penetrate through the mystery of this confession.

Of course, it is frequently objected that the Scriptures nowhere use the terms "Triune" or "Trinity," and that therefore the doctrine is a confessional or theological construction which is not biblically warranted or required. This objection is contradicted by many passages in the Scriptures which speak expressly of the Father, the Son, and the Holy Spirit (Matt. 28:19; 2 Cor. 13:14; Luke 3:21,22; 1 Cor. 12:4-6; 1 Pet. 1:2), or affirm directly the deity of the Son (Matt. 11:27; 16:16; 26:63,64; John 1:1,18; Rom. 9:5; 1 Cor. 2:8; 2 Cor. 5:10; Phil. 2:6; Col. 2:9; Heb. 1:1-3; Rev. 19:16) or the Spirit (Acts 5:3-4; 1 Cor. 3:16; 1 Cor. 2:10-11; Heb. 9:14; John 3:5-6).

But this denial of the Trinity also contradicts the heart of our confession as Christians — that in the person and work of the Father, the Son, and the Holy Spirit, the Triune God has truly revealed Himself. Such a denial amounts to saying that God is not eternally in Himself of the same character as He has in His own

---

[10]*Ecumenical Creeds and Reformed Confessions*, pp. 5-6.

good-pleasure revealed Himself to be in relation to us. Any denial of the Trinity is, therefore, a denial of the gospel. For if the true and living God is not eternally the Father of the Son in the fellowship of the Holy Spirit, then we do not know Him nor in knowing Him do we have eternal life. Then, we cannot be certain that the Son has been sent by the Father to make Him known to us (John 1:1-18).

Another way in which this could be expressed is to say that the Christian believes that God was the Almighty Father before He purposed to adopt us for Christ's sake to be His children. He is eternally the Father of the only-begotten Son (2 Cor. 1:3). But when we become His children through Christ, He graciously adopts us as His own and grants us to share in the privilege of sonship (1 John 3:1; Rom. 8:15,29 Eph. 1:5). The love which He has eternally for His Son is revealed to and shared with us. Our assurance that the Father loves us is rooted in His willingness to share with us something of that love with which He has eternally loved the Son in the fellowship of the Spirit.

This means that we cannot know God the Father apart from the response of faith to His Word and to the revelation of Himself through the Son and in the power of the Spirit. There is no true knowledge of the Triune God apart from the response of faith to that which He has revealed concerning Himself through the Word become flesh and the Scriptures in their testimony to Him. Those who speak, therefore, of their knowledge of a "god" through some other means or in terms which ignore or deny the Trinity, speak out of their vain and sinful imagination. There is no knowledge of the only God, the Triune God, apart from a knowledge of His Son and the inward illumination of His Spirit (1 Cor. 2:1-13).

The Almighty Maker of heaven and earth

It is noteworthy that the Creed, though it is thoroughly Trinitarian in its confession of our faith in God, focuses always on the works of the Triune God in creation and redemption. The Creed is not interested in an abstract consideration of who God is. It is interested in the manner of God's revelation of Himself in

His works and in the covenant relationship or fellowship between Him and His people.

In this first article of the Creed, the focus is upon God the Father's work as the "Almighty, Maker of heaven and earth." This is the biblical point of departure for any confession of God and His works. God the Father, the eternal Father of our Lord Jesus Christ and our Father for Christ's sake, is the sovereign Creator of all things, visible and invisible. He is the One who has created all things and who sustains them in being.

One way in which the church has affirmed its faith in God the Father as the Creator of heaven and earth, is by the doctrine of "creation out of nothing" (*creatio ex nihilo*). According to the biblical record of creation, God created all things in heaven and on earth by the Word of His power (Gen. 1 & 2). As the Psalmist describes it, "By the word of the Lord the heavens were made, and by the breath of His mouth all their host" (Psalm 32:6; cf. Job 26:13; 33:4; Isa. 40:12,13; John 1:3; 1 Cor. 8:6; Col. 1:15-17). Nothing antedated or preceded this act of creation through the Creator's Word. God sovereignly and freely called into existence a world that had no previous existence in any form whatsoever. Accordingly, we read in Hebrews 11:3, "By faith we understand that the worlds were prepared by the word of God, so that what is seen was not made out of things which are visible." There was no primordial mass which God simply ordered. God alone, in radical distinction from the creature, has neither beginning nor ending of days. He alone is eternal in the heavens, the Almighty Maker of heaven and earth.

Luther, in his meditation on God's sovereign and gracious work in creation, once remarked that this confession is in many respects more difficult to understand than the confession of the eternal Son's becoming flesh for our salvation. For when we confess that God created all things by the Word of His mouth "out of nothing," we are saying that God has done something for which there is and could be absolutely no analogy in our experience. To confess that God created out of nothing all things by His own will and power is, therefore, one way in which to confess His transcendence and holiness. The only kind of creativity or making which we know from our experience involves taking something pre-existing and giving it a particular shape or form. Such creativity — whether expressed in the building of a house, the sculpting of a sculpture, the writing of a novel or poem — is radically different from creating something out of nothing!

The prophet Isaiah speaks appropriately, therefore, on behalf of the Lord, when he declares, "'To whom then will you liken Me, that I should be his equal?,' says the Holy One. Lift up your eyes on high and see who has created these stars, the One who leads forth their host by number. He calls them all by name; because of the greatness of His might and the strength of His power, not one of them is missing" (Isa. 40:25,26).

The Christian confesses that the eternal God and Father of our Lord Jesus Christ — whom we dare by faith to call our Father for Christ's sake — is this great and holy Creator. He is the sovereign Creator who called all things into existence by the Word of His power, and who directs all things by His eternal counsel and providence.

The implications of this confession

For the believer's comfort

Any reflection upon this confession must begin with the comfort which follows upon the knowledge that God is the Father Almighty. Those who by faith confess that they believe in God the Father Almighty, Maker of heaven and earth, know that they are not only creatures whom He has created, but children whom He loves for Christ, His Son's, sake. This is the foundation upon which their comfort and hope, both in life and death, is built.

The Heidelberg Catechism, in its summary of what we believe in this first article of the Creed, stresses this comfort by noting two things.[11] First, we confess in this article that the Father is

---

[11]In answer to the question, "What do you believe when you say: 'I believe in God the Father, Almighty, Maker of heaven and earth'?," this Catechism declares: "That the eternal Father of our Lord Jesus Christ, who out of nothing created heaven and earth and everything in them, who still upholds and rules them by his eternal counsel and providence, is my God and Father because of Christ his Son. I trust him so much that I do not doubt he will provide whatever I need for body and soul, and he will turn to my good whatever

Almighty God. He is able — as the Creator of all things, as the Sovereign Lord of history, as the Providential Sustainer and Governor of what He has created — to do all His holy will. Nothing whatsoever is able to stand in the way or to frustrate His counsel and purpose. Second, we confess that Almighty God is a Faithful Father. The love of the Father for those who belong through faith to Christ is a sure and faithful love. The love of the Father in heaven for His children is such that He will not fail to accomplish His purpose in their salvation. Of this they may be certain!

This is the marvelous comfort of our faith in God the Father Almighty. We can confess in the words of the Heidelberg Catechism, "I trust Him so much that I do not doubt He will provide whatever I need for body and soul, and He will turn to my good whatever adversity He sends me in this sad world" (Lord's Day 9).

For the rejection of evolution

The issue of creation and evolution is also unavoidably addressed by this article of our Christian confession. No one who seriously reflects upon the implications of this confession of faith in God the Father, Almighty, Maker of heaven and earth, may ignore this issue.

Many have attempted to marry the Christian confession of God's creation of all things by the Word of His power with the theory of evolution. This marriage is commonly termed "theistic evolution" or "creationomic science." God is said to be the Creator, but He employs the means of evolution to accomplish His purpose in creation. The Christian confession of God as Creator is said to be a *religious confession*, focused upon the question of God's "external relation" to the creation. The theory of evolution is a *scientific theory*, focused upon the question of the

adversity he sends me in this sad world. He is able to do this because he is almighty God; he desires to do this because he is a faithful Father" (*Ecumenical Creeds and Reformed Confessions*, p. 15).

"internal relations" that obtain between creaturely entities. The two *complement* one another and can easily be harmonized.

The problem with this apparent resolution of the difference between the Christian doctrine of creation and the scientific doctrine of evolution, is that it glosses over the real incompatibility between them. The theory of (macro) evolution, because it aims to provide an account of the origin of the universe in its present form and of the evolutionary development of the human race, denies that which the Christian doctrine of creation confesses. It denies the Christian confession that God created all things out of nothing by His Word, "good and perfect" from the beginning. Creation is redefined as an on-going and continuous evolutionary process, so that the difference between God's act of creation and His providential superintendence of what He has created is blurred.

Consequently, it is impossible on an evolutionary basis to affirm that the creation was called forth by the Word of God in an originally complete and perfect form. Yet, this is precisely what the Scriptures teach and the confessions affirm! It is interesting to observe that the Heidelberg Catechism speaks here of the "eternal Father of our Lord Jesus Christ, who out of nothing created heaven and earth and everything in them" (Lord's Day 9). The Belgic Confession is even more explicit, when it says, "We believe that the Father by the Word, that is, by His Son, has created of nothing the heaven, the earth, and all creatures, when it seemed good unto Him, giving unto every creature its being, shape, form, and several offices to serve its Creator" (Article 12).[12] Neither one of these confessions can be harmonized with the doctrine of evolution, which teaches that God did not create all creatures in the beginning according to their particular form and office.

It must also be observed here that the doctrine of evolution operates upon a naturalistic premise that is inimical to the Christian confession of creation and the comfort which follows upon that confession. Simply stated, the doctrine of evolution teaches that at every time and place, so far as the internal functioning and life of creaturely entities is concerned, all things

[12]*Ecumenical Creeds and Reformed Confessions*, p. 68.

invariably act according to scientifically observable and verifiable "laws" or "regularities." There may be no exceptions to this rule.

The problem with this premise is its naturalism. It virtually denies, so far as the development of the creation is concerned, the very thing which is most essential to a Christian doctrine of creation — that the Creator is not subject to the limits of the creation when He creates all things or sovereignly accomplishes all things according to His counsel. God the Father is not only able to create all things — He has! And He is not only able to do all things necessary to the accomplishment of His counsel in creation and history — He will! This Christian doctrine of creation and also of God's powerful works in redemption (including those works which are "supernatural" or "miraculous") strikes like an axe at the root of the tree of all evolutionary theories which operate upon a naturalistic basis.

For our language

There is one other implication which needs to be addressed today in connection with this first article of the Creed. And that is the issue of the language we are to use when we speak about God. Many Christian believers, influenced by the spirit and forms of contemporary feminism, have sought to alter their language when they speak about God. They are reluctant or even unwilling to speak of the "Father," the "Son," or to use the pronoun "He" in reference to God. Moreover, they have self-consciously created new forms of language for our speaking about God which are "gender-inclusive" and acceptable by the standards of feminism. For example, it is suggested that we should speak about God as "our Mother" or that we should conceive of the Holy Spirit as the "feminine" member of the Trinity. Arguments are advanced and strategies are adopted to rid our Bible translations, lectionaries and song-books of their allegedly "sexist" bias in the language employed with respect to God.

How are we to respond to this endeavor, which has become so much a part of the life of the churches today? What does the Christian's historic and common confession, "I believe in God the Father Almighty, Maker of heaven and earth," have to say in connection with this issue of the language we use when we speak about God in worship and confession?

It should be admitted, of course, that this movement has been an occasion for a renewed appreciation of the truth that the Triune God is neither male nor female, and that He is not revealed to us as though He were subject to the kind of creaturely differences which characterize men and women as His image-bearers. Similarly, the pressing of this issue has served to remind us that the Scriptures use images which compare God's dealings with His people to the tender care and nurture which a mother displays toward her children (cf. Isaiah 49:14,15; Matt. 24:37).

Nevertheless, this attempt to alter the language of our confession about God "the Father" Almighty is fundamentally unbiblical and idolatrous. Any time we seek self-consciously to speak about God and to know Him in ways which are not taught us in His Word, we are guilty of devising an idol, a "god" of our imagining. The first two commandments expressly forbid our devising or imagining any other God than the true and living God, who is pleased to reveal Himself in His Word to His people.

Therefore, we must confess our faith in the Triune God in terms which are born out of a careful listening and submission to Scripture. We are not permitted arrogantly and presumptuously, thinking ourselves wiser than God Himself, to speak of Him in any other manner than He has taught us in His Word. This requires us to confess our faith in Him according to the standard of the Creed. For the Creed rightly seeks to re-iterate what God has revealed about Himself in the Scriptures and insists that He is truly known in these terms alone!

Conclusion

This first and fundamental article of the Creed is one which must constantly be affirmed and re-affirmed by the Christian believer. Do we know and believe in the Father Almighty, the eternal Father of the Son, who is our Father for Christ's sake? Do we believe that He is the Almighty Maker of heaven and earth? That He created all things out of nothing by the Word of His mouth? That he will not fail of His sovereign good-pleasure in all the works of His hands? That He is the One who comforts us in all the circumstances of our lives?

Recommended reading:

Bavinck, Herman. *The Doctrine of God*. Trans. by W. Hendriksen. Edinburgh and Carlisle, PA: Banner of Truth, 1977 [reprint of 1951 ed.].

McGrath, Alister E. *Understanding the Trinity*. Grand Rapids, MI: Zondervan, 1988.

Questions for Discussion

1. What is meant by the "Trinitarian structure" of the Apostles' Creed?

2. The most common way of describing the Trinity is to say that God is "one in essence or being, three in person." As much as you are able, explain what is meant by this language? How does this doctrine differ from "tritheism"? "Unitarianism"?

3. How would you defend the doctrine of the Trinity from the Scriptures? How would you answer the objection of someone who would say, "but the word, 'trinity,' is not even used in the Bible"?

4. What "analogies" have sometimes been used to explain how God can be one being, yet existing eternally in three Persons? Can you think of any others? Do such analogies finally explain the doctrine of the Trinity?

5. What is meant by speaking of creation "out of nothing" (*creatio ex nihilo*)? Why is it important to say that nothing pre-existed the creation (except the Triune God, of course)?

6. What is the difference between the Christian doctrine of creation and "pantheism"?

7. Why are the doctrine of creation and the theory of evolution incompatible?

8. What is the difference between creation and providence?

9. What are the implications of the Christian doctrine of the Trinity for the kind of language we use to speak of God? Why may we not address God as "our Father and Mother"?

CHAPTER THREE

"AND IN JESUS CHRIST,
HIS ONLY BEGOTTEN SON, OUR LORD"

"And you shall call His name Jesus, for it is He who will save His people from their sins." Matthew 1:21

"He said to them, 'But who do you say that I am?' And Simon Peter answered and said, 'Thou art the Christ, the Son of the living God.'" Matthew 16:15,16

The second article of the Apostles' Creed, in which the Christian believer confesses his faith in "Jesus Christ, His [the Father's] only begotten Son, our Lord," confronts us with the same difficulty we faced in considering the first article. How do we say all that needs to be said about this article? And how do we avoid saying things that inadequately express what this article, in a terse, yet comprehensive way, says about the person and work of our Lord Jesus Christ?

The difficulty goes deeper than that, however, because no one can even make this confession about our Lord Jesus Christ unless the Father reveal it to him. It is noteworthy that in Matthew 16, when Jesus Himself asked his disciples, "But who do you say that I am?," he ascribed Peter's confession, "Thou art the Christ; the Son of the living God," to the direct revelation of the Father. And so we read, "Jesus answered and said to him, 'Blessed are you,

Simon Barjona, because flesh and blood did not reveal this to you, but My Father who is in heaven" (Matt. 16:17).

This, of course, holds true for the entirety of what we believe as Christians on the basis of the Word of God. No one could believe and confess apart from God's gracious self-disclosure and revelation of Himself to His people. But nowhere does this come to sharper and more profound expression than in connection with the confession we make about the only begotten Son, our Lord Jesus Christ. Only when the Father through revelation opens our eyes to see Him in all of His glory, the glory of His person and work, are we able to make this confession of faith from the heart (compare 2 Cor. 4:3,4).

And so we approach this second article of the creed with humility and reverence, knowing that we have to do here once again with things only known by us through divine revelation. What we with joy confess about the Lord Jesus Christ are things of which it must be said, "Things which eye has not seen and ear has not heard, and which have not entered the heart of man, all that God has prepared for those who love him" (1 Cor. 2:9).

Jesus

The first word employed in this second article to describe the only begotten Son is the name "Jesus." Before even saying or affirming anything about His eternal sonship and deity, we confess that our Lord Jesus Christ bears a proper name which is uniquely and especially His.

To appreciate the significance of this name, "Jesus," with which anyone acquainted with the gospel is so familiar, we need to be reminded of the function a person's name often served in the biblical writings and the circumstances which attended the "naming" of Jesus.

We are not accustomed to the practice in which names often serve to identify or disclose a person's character and work. Consequently, when we hear the expression, "What's in a name?," we are not surprised, because so often there is little to the names we choose for our children. In our society, names often are only "labels" that distinguish us from others. After all, you have to have a name, if you hope to obtain a credit card or a social security card or avoid being confused with others. But in the biblical writings, names tell a story. They unveil or reveal who someone is, the nature of his work or task. Names in the Bible often proclaim a message and indicate the Lord's purpose which will be accomplished through the one named.

This is supremely true when it comes to the name "Jesus." This name — which in the Greek language of the New Testament is equivalent to the Hebrew name, "Joshua," in the Old Testament — means "he who saves" or simply "savior." When the birth of our Lord was announced by the angel to Joseph in Matthew 1, special emphasis is given to His naming — "And you shall call His name Jesus, for it is He who will save His people from their sins" (Matt. 1:21). For this reason, in the subsequent account of Jesus' circumcision, it is emphasized that He was "called Jesus, the name given by the angel before He was conceived in the womb" (Luke 2:21).

What a remarkable story is proclaimed by our Lord's name! By means of His name, a name which was divinely appointed for Him, we are told that He is in His person and work the embodiment of the fullness of salvation. Through Him there is given to us salvation from the power, the dominion and the consequence of sin. In our confession of His name, then, we acknowledge that in Him alone we discover a complete and perfect Savior, One whose saving work accomplishes all that is necessary for us sinners. We confess in the words of the apostle Paul in 1 Timothy 1:15, "It is a trustworthy saying, deserving full acceptance, that Christ Jesus came into the world to save sinners, among whom I am the chief."

Of course, to confess our Lord's name sincerely demands of us that we find in Him alone, and not in ourselves or in any other, our salvation. It demands from us that we boast alone in Him and not in ourselves or in our own works or accomplishments. Furthermore it demands that we recognize the terrible character of our sin as lawless rebellion against the will of the Creator, rebellion which necessarily provokes God's wrath and judgment upon us. It is to confess that our real sickness which would, but for the grace of our Savior, lead to eternal death, is the sickness of our sin. We confess that the only remedy for us sinners is to be found in the Savior who bears the name "Jesus."

It is worth pausing for a moment to ponder this. In the midst of a secular world which denies the reality of sin, minimizes its consequence, and seeks salvation in a variety of political and economic ideologies, the Christian believer confesses the name of "Jesus." We confess that "there is salvation in no one else; for there is no other name under heaven that has been given among men, by which we must be saved" (Acts 4:12).

Christ

If the name "Jesus" identifies who He is in the great work which He accomplishes, the second word, "Christ," is a title which serves to remind us of our Savior's office or task. If the name "Jesus" describes our Lord as the only Savior, the title "Christ" describes the work He was called to do in order to be our Savior.

The word "Christ" is the New Testament equivalent of "Messiah" or "Anointed One" in the Old Testament. Because we are so accustomed to speaking of our "Lord Jesus Christ," we are not often conscious of the fact that we might better and more biblically speak of "Christ Jesus," or even more literally, of "the Messiah, Jesus." For, when we describe our Lord as the Christ, we are confessing that He was ordained by the Father and anointed by the Holy Spirit to a particular task or calling. Just as the Old Testament prophets, priests and kings were ordained by God and (at least in the instance of the priests and the kings) anointed with oil, an anointing which symbolized their being set aside for and endowed with the Spirit for service, so our Lord was commissioned by the Father and empowered by the Spirit for His office and work. It is for this reason that we read in the gospel accounts of our Lord's baptism, that the Spirit of God descended as a dove and came upon Him and the Father declared concerning Him, "This is My beloved Son, in whom I am well-pleased" (Matt. 3:16,16; compare Mark 1:10,11; Luke 3:21,22).

Specifically, our confession that Jesus is the "Christ" means that we acknowledge Him to have been ordained to a threefold office or work. In the Heidelberg Catechism, Lord's Day 12, we have a biblically informed and beautiful statement of this threefold office of our Lord:

> He has been ordained by God the Father and has been anointed with the Holy Spirit to be our chief prophet and teacher who perfectly reveals to us the secret counsel and will of God for our deliverance; our only high priest who has set us free by the one sacrifice of His body, and who continually pleads our cause with the Father; and our eternal king who governs us by His Word and Spirit, and who guards us and keeps us in the freedom He has won for us.[13]

As our chief prophet and teacher, Christ was ordained by the Father and anointed by the Spirit to preach the gospel of the kingdom, to reveal through His own teaching and the ministry of His apostles the fullness of the gospel. He is the "Word" become flesh (John 1), whose words are life and truth for they are the words which the Father gave Him to speak (John 8). He is the prophet who was to come (Deut. 18:15; compare Hebrews 1; Acts 3:23). Not only did He reveal the Word of God during the course of His ministry upon the earth, but He also continues to minister His Word through the Spirit-inspired testimony of the apostles, inscripturated for us in the New Testament (John 14:26; 16:12-14; Eph. 2:20; 4:11; 1 Thess. 2:13). When we read the Scriptures or the Word is preached to us, we hear the voice of our chief prophet who shepherds His people by means of His Word (John 10:1-5).

As our only high priest, Christ was ordained by the Father and anointed by the Spirit to fulfill perfectly the office of priest, making sacrifice for the sins of His people and interceding on their behalf before the Father. In the New Testament, this priestly office of Christ is pervasively taught, but nowhere so fully and comprehensively as in the book of Hebrews. Christ is our only high priest in that He has offered a sacrifice of Himself once for all, which perfectly accomplishes and effects the cleansing from sin

---

[13]*Ecumenical Creeds and Reformed Confessions*, p. 18.

which was only foreshadowed and typified under the sacrificial system of the Old Testament (e.g. Hebrews 7:26-8:6). On the basis of His perfect, once-for-all sacrifice, He is able to make continual and effective intercession on behalf of all those for whom He offered Himself. He is the "lamb of God who takes away the sins of the world" (John 1:29), "our Passover" (1 Cor. 5:7), who "Himself bore our sins in His body on the cross, that we might die to sin and live to righteousness" (1 Peter 2:24).

And as our eternal king, Christ not only proclaimed the gospel of the kingdom, but He is even now establishing His kingdom in the earth through the Spirit and Word. After having been crucified and raised from the dead, He has ascended to the Father's right hand and been granted the power and authority to receive the nations as His rightful inheritance (Matt. 28:18). He has vanquished the power of sin and death, set at flight the evil one and all his host, and will not fail to bring all things into subjection to Himself (1 Cor. 15:24-28). As the Mighty King and Lord, He will not fail to keep and defend His people against all their enemies and secure the ultimate consummation of the kingdom in glory.

To confess that Jesus is the "Christ," therefore, also confronts us with several questions. If, as we confess, Christ is our chief prophet, do we find ourselves humbly listening to His voice as He speaks to us through the Scriptures or through the preaching of His Word? If, as we confess, Christ is our only high priest, do we trust that by means of His one sacrifice upon the cross for our sins and continued intercession for us at the Father's right hand, we have peace with God? And if, as we confess, Christ is our eternal King, are we gladly subject to His Word and Spirit in our seeking of His kingdom and battle against the kingdom of darkness and sin?

The Only-begotten Son

From the identification of our Savior by his name, "Jesus," and his title, "Christ," we move to confess what is most marvelous about this One whom we call Jesus Christ — He is none other than the "only begotten Son." He is the eternal Son of the Father who became man in order that He might be our Savior and fulfill the work to which His Father ordained Him and for which the Spirit empowered Him.[14]

In this expression the Creed affirms that the person of our Lord Jesus Christ is one and the same with the Person of the only begotten Son who is true and eternal God, together with the Father and the Holy Spirit. Its use of the language, "only begotten," serves to emphasize that it was the eternal and natural Son of God, the Son who dwells eternally with the Father and the Spirit, who became incarnate for us and for our salvation by assuming our human nature. Against every ancient and contemporary denial of His deity, the Creed declares that He is fully equal and one in essence with the Father and the Spirit. He is, to use the words of the Nicene Creed, "... begotten of the Father before all worlds; God of God, Light of Light, very God of very God; begotten, not made, being of one substance with the Father, by whom all things were made."[15]

In its classical formulation, the Christian church has confessed the doctrine of the Person of our Lord Jesus Christ by saying that He is "one and the same Son, our Lord Jesus Christ, the same perfect in Godhead and also perfect in manhood; truly God and truly man" (The Chalcedon Creed, 451 A.D.).[16] In making this confession, we do not pretend arrogantly to comprehend the

---

[14]It is unfortunate that some recent translations of the Creed use the language "only" Son, rather than "only begotten" Son. Though the oldest Latin forms of the Apostle's Creed do use the expression, *unicum Filium* (lit. "only Son"), it was early in the transmission of the Creed that the preferred and received language of *unigenitum Filium* (lit. "only begotten Son") was used. This not only better corresponds to the traditional translation of the Greek term used in the gospel of John (*monogenees*; John 1:18; 3:16), but it also better reflects the consensus of the universal church on the deity of the Son (who is said in the Nicene Creed to be "begotten, not made," in a direct attack upon the heresy of Arius and the Arians who denied the full deity and co-equality of the Son with the Father). Moreover, the translation, "only Son," says something which is, strictly speaking, not true! Though Jesus Christ is the only "natural" Son of the Father, those who through faith are engrafted into Him and indwelt by His Spirit are also sons and daughters, children of the Father in heaven (Rom. 8:15; Gal. 4:4-6; 1 John 3:1). This newer translation, regrettably, blurs this highly important truth.

[15]*Creeds and Confessions*, p. 4.

[16]Philip Schaff, *The Creeds of Christendom*, vol. II, p. 62.

mystery of the Person of our Lord. Rather, we seek with humility to say what must be said concerning Him — that in our Lord Jesus Christ, the Son of God has come to us, assumed our human nature, in order that He might accomplish our salvation.

The church constantly faces here the temptation to deny or compromise the deity of the Son or to deny or compromise the genuineness of His humanity. Both, however, are clearly taught in Scripture and both must be affirmed to preserve the biblical revelation concerning His person. Though it is common today to assume the humanity of Christ and to treat His deity as though it were in question, the Scriptures cannot be understood without acknowledging that it was the eternal Son who was incarnate in the person of our Lord Jesus Christ. His humanity is everywhere taught and proclaimed (e.g.: John 8:40; Acts 2:22; Rom. 5:15; 1 Cor. 15:21; 1 Tim. 2:5). But so is His deity (Matt. 11:27; 16:16; 26:63,64; John 1:1,18; 1 Cor. 2:8; Phil. 2:6; Col. 2:9; Heb. 1:1-3). In neither instance is it a matter of simple appealing to an isolated proof-text here or there. The Scriptures throughout record the story of our Lord Jesus Christ as the story of God's, the eternal Son's, entrance into our humanity and history in order to redeem us.

This is also the reason the confession of Christ's deity as the only begotten Son is the heart of our confession as Christian believers. The whole of our confession, the ground of our hope whether in life or in death, the thing that gives us "joy unspeakable and full of glory," is just this — that "God was in Christ reconciling the world to Himself"! Or as it is expressed in Romans 8:31,32, "What then shall we say to these things? If God is for us, who is against us? He who did not spare His own Son, but delivered Him up for us all, how will He not also with Him freely give us all things?"

Our Lord

It is only fitting that the second article concludes with the expression, "our Lord." This is the fruit of all that has already been confessed concerning Him. Probably for this reason, Luther, in his summary of what we confess in this second article of the

Creed, placed the emphasis upon the confession of Christ's Lordship: "I believe that Jesus Christ, true God born of the Father in eternity, and also true man born of the Virgin Mary, is my Lord."

But what are we confessing with these words, "our Lord"? Here too our familiarity with the words may prevent our appreciating the force of what we are confessing. To confess that Jesus Christ, the only begotten Son, is "our Lord," is to confess that we belong to Him because He has claimed and purchased us for Himself. He is the Lord who loved us and gave Himself up for us, that He might purchase us as His cherished possession (Gal. 2:20). We belong to Him!

The confession of Christ's lordship is comprised, then, of two parts. On the one hand, it expresses the blessed truth that we have been purchased by Christ at the cost, not of silver or gold, but of his precious blood (1 Peter 1:18,19; Col. 1:13,14; Heb. 2:14,15). We now enjoy a liberty in belonging to Him that contrasts radically with our former slavery to sin and oppression under the tyranny of the devil. We belong to Jesus Christ, our faithful Savior! And on the other hand, it means that we live consciously, in all aspects of our life, in the awareness that "whether we live or whether we die, we are the Lord's" (Rom. 14:8). Therefore, we make it our ambition in life to please Him (2 Cor. 5:9), to do what is in keeping with our status as His possession.

So much more could be said. And certainly it could be said in a better and more adequate way. But this will have to suffice for us in our brief review of this article in the Creed. The words of Charles Wesley's well-known hymn summarize the whole of it well:

O for a thousand tongues to sing, My Great Redeemer's praise; The glories of my God and King, The Triumphs of His grace.

My gracious Master and my God, O help me to proclaim; To spread through all the earth abroad, The honors of Thy Name.

Jesus! the Name that charms our fears, That bids our sorrows cease; 'Tis music in the sinner's ear, 'Tis life and health and peace. Amen.

Recommended reading:

Berkouwer, Gerrit C. *The Person of Christ.* Grand Rapids, MI: Eerdmans, 1954.

Runia, Klaas. *The Present-Day Christological Debate.* Downers Grove, IL: Intervarsity, 1984.

Wells, David F. *The Person of Christ.* Westchester, IL: Crossway Books, 1984.

Questions for Discussion

1. Identify and discuss the biblical meaning and Old Testament background of the name "Jesus." Do you believe it is wise or proper for parents today to give their children the name Jesus?

2. Give examples of modern denials of salvation through Jesus Christ alone. How does Acts 4:12 confirm the meaning of Jesus' name?

3. Explain the meaning of Jesus' title, the "Christ." Describe the Old Testament background for this title.

4. What is meant by the three-fold office of Christ?

5. In the Nicene Creed, it is said that Jesus Christ was "begotten, not made." What is the difference between confessing that Jesus is the "only-begotten" Son of the Father or that He was "made" by the Father? What cults today believe that Christ was "made" or "created"?

6. Defend from the Bible the confession that Jesus is one person with two complete natures, divine and human.

7. When the Apostles' Creed adds that Jesus Christ is "our Lord," what does this tell us about our relationship as Christians to Jesus Christ?

8. How does the lordship of Jesus Christ affect the following areas of our lives: education, politics, economics, entertainment? Be specific.

CHAPTER FOUR

"WHO WAS CONCEIVED BY THE HOLY SPIRIT, BORN OF THE VIRGIN MARY"

"And Mary said to the angel, 'How can this be, since I am a virgin?' And the angel answered and said to her, 'The Holy Spirit will come upon you, and the power of the Most High will overshadow you; and for that reason the holy offspring shall be called the Son of God." Luke 1:34-35

One of the significant features of the modernist-fundamentalist controversy of the first decades of the twentieth century was the publication of a series of booklets, entitled *The Fundamentals*, which set forth the fundamentals of the historic Christian faith over against the errors of modernism. The first article in the first booklet was written by James Orr of Scotland on "The Virgin Birth of Christ." That this was the first "fundamental" of the faith addressed in this series should come as no surprise. For the church's confession of Christ's birth in the Apostles' Creed, that He was "conceived by the Holy Spirit, born of the virgin Mary," has been one of the most commonly rejected articles of the Creed among liberal theologians and churches in the nineteenth and twentieth centuries.

Unhappily, this is often the issue which occupies our attention, when we consider what the Creed says about the great miracle of the incarnation of our Lord Jesus Christ. We focus attention upon the offense of this confession to unbelief, and we neglect the joy which should be ours in the confession of our Savior's birth. We expend too much effort in the defense of this confession, and not enough in the exposition of its meaning and significance.

It is true, of course, that we must defend the confession we make here. We cannot condone the unholy mockery of unbelief when it refuses to join Mary and the confessing church of all ages in saying, "My soul exalts the Lord, and my spirit has rejoiced in God my Savior. ... He has done mighty deeds with His arm; He has scattered those who were proud in the thoughts of their heart" (Luke 1:46,51). Over against those who will not embrace this great miracle of our Lord's conception by the Holy Spirit and birth of the virgin Mary, we must insist upon this article of our faith and do battle with every form of arrogance which exalts itself against the Lord and His Word. To do so is not, as some would suggest, to fall prey to a fundamentalism without depth or breadth. It is only to insist that this is legitimately a fundamental article of our faith, as this faith is summarized in the Apostles' Creed.

But what we must especially focus upon is the meaning of this confession. What are we confessing when we say this? And why is this article so important a part of our confession that it finds its place as the first thing that needs to be said about the work of our Lord Jesus Christ?

The means of our Lord's incarnation

This article of the Creed is the first in a series which describe a variety of acts or deeds of our Lord Jesus Christ — He was conceived, born, suffered, crucified, buried, descended, rose again, seated on the right hand of God, and will come again. Whereas the previous article gives us a summary statement of who our Savior is — He is "Jesus Christ, the only begotten Son, our Lord" — this article begins to tell the story of what He has done to accomplish His saving work.

This story of our Savior's saving work begins appropriately with the event of His birth. The eternal Word became flesh and dwelt among us by means of His miraculous conception by the Holy Spirit and birth of the virgin Mary. It was in this way that the eternal Son of God assumed our human nature and became

man, a real man who was and is like us in every respect, yet
without sin. This is the great miracle of Christmas, the miracle in
which the eternal Word became flesh for us and for our salvation
(John 1).

What should impress us in this confession concerning Christ's
birth is the way it which it calls attention to its unique and definite
character. The uniqueness of Christ's person as true God and true
man is mirrored in the uniqueness of the manner of His birth.
Though in becoming one with us He was born as all of us are
born (compare Gal. 4:4, "God sent forth His Son, born of a
woman"), He was born by way of a special miracle. He was
"conceived by the Holy Spirit, born of the virgin Mary." Thus, the
greatness of the miracle of God's becoming one with us finds an
appropriate reflection in the uniqueness of the circumstances of
His birth.

Notice first the words "conceived by the Holy Spirit." These
words alert us to the truth that the child born from Mary's womb
was born of God. He owes His life to the fact that in Him God in
person became man. The miraculous conception of this child
through the operation of the Holy Spirit testifies to the uniqueness of His person as true and eternal Son of God. We should not
mistakenly take these words, therefore, to mean that the Holy
Spirit was the Father of Jesus Christ. Strictly speaking, they simply
affirm that the child conceived in Mary's womb has no earthly
father and that in His conception we have to do with an act of
God's power and grace through the Holy Spirit.

We are reminded and taught through this confession, then,
that this child was no ordinary child. For, in this quite unique and
definite circumstance of His conception by the Holy Spirit, we
have a circumstance that perfectly fits with the uniqueness and
definiteness of His person. How fitting it is that, when the eternal
Son of God became one with us in the incarnation, He should do
so by way of this holy conception by the Holy Spirit. What could
have been more in keeping with the uniqueness of His person as
the Son of God, than that He should have been become incarnate
under these circumstances? This is also emphasized by the angel's
words to Mary herself, "... and for that reason the holy offspring
shall be called the Son of God" (Luke 1:35).

Equally striking are the words "born of the Virgin Mary." These words are simple to understand, yet staggering in their implication.

Though they also testify to the truth that He was conceived by the Holy Spirit — that His mother was a virgin and therefore He had no human father — they especially underscore the great mystery of His becoming altogether one with us, even one of us, our brother! He was born, just as we are born. He came to share in our "flesh and blood" (compare Hebrews 2:9-21). He "emptied Himself, taking the form of a bond-servant, being made in the likeness of men" (Phil. 2:7).

And so we have in this article a confession about the birth of Him whom we confess to be true God and true man. The circumstances of His birth by means of a holy conception and a virgin mother eloquently testify to the uniqueness of His person.

The holiness of our Mediator

However, this article does not only speak of the manner of our Lord's incarnation. It also speaks of His sanctity and holiness as our Mediator. There is in the circumstance of His being conceived by the Holy Spirit a testimony to His being set apart from the moment of His conception as one who was holy and without sin of any kind.

Whereas all of us are "born and conceived in sin," Jesus Christ was born and conceived without sin. He was, not only in the life of obedience which he lived and the work which He performed, but also in His conception and from his birth, set apart from sinners in being personally sinless and holy. This sinlessness and holiness of our Lord Jesus Christ is absolutely indispensable to His saving work on behalf of sinners. Unless He was himself sinless and perfect in every way, He could not offer His obedience or His sacrifice for others in a way that would be perfectly sufficient and adequate to their need. He could not cleanse His people, if He was Himself unclean. Nor could He substitute Himself as a perfect and unblemished sacrifice for sinners, were He Himself a sinner.

One does not have to read far in the New Testament to discover the importance of Christ's holiness and sinlessness to the accomplishment of His saving work. This is evident from the emphasis upon His perfect obedience and holiness. He came to fulfill all righteousness (Matt. 3:15). He knew no sin (2 Cor. 5:21). He "committed no sin, nor was any deceit found in His mouth" (1 Peter 2:22). Or, as the apostle John expresses it, "And you know that He appeared in order to take away sins; and in Him there is no sin" (1 John 3:5).

Because of His sinlessness and perfect holiness, Christ was able to make atonement for the sins of His people. He not only kept the whole law for us, but He also suffered its penalty on our behalf. Unlike the first Adam, whose one act of disobedience brought condemnation and death, Christ, the second Adam, by His one act of obedience brings righteousness and life (Rom. 5:12-21). He was able to die for us, "the just for the unjust, in order that He might bring us to God" (1 Pet. 3:18).

The importance of Christ's holiness for his saving work on our behalf is expressed clearly in the book of Hebrews.

> For it was fitting that we should have such a high priest, holy, innocent, undefiled, separated from sinners and exalted above the heavens; who does not need daily, like those high priests, to offer up sacrifices, first for His own sins, and then for the sins of the people, because this He did once for all when he offered up Himself. (Heb. 7:26-27)

> For if the blood of goats and bulls and the ashes of a heifer sprinkling those who have been defiled, satisfy for the cleansing of the flesh, how much more will the blood of Christ, who through the eternal Spirit offered Himself without blemish to God, cleanse your conscience from dead works to serve the living God. (Heb. 9:13-14)

Because Christ's work as priestly Mediator requires that He represent an unholy people before a holy God, it was necessary that He Himself be perfectly holy and be able to make sacrifice of Himself for His people.

In the Heidelberg Catechism, this feature of Christ's conception by the Holy Spirit is especially emphasized. To the question, "How does the holy conception and birth of Christ benefit you," the Catechism answers, "He is our mediator, and with his innocence and perfect holiness he removes from God's sight my sin — mine since I was conceived."[17] By virtue of our Lord's conception by the Holy Spirit, He was separated from sin as holy from birth and able to be the Savior of His people.[18]

A sign of sovereign grace

Before considering briefly the way in which this article in the Creed has been misused to exalt inordinately the virgin Mary, I would also like to take note of one other aspect of this unique birth of our Lord which merits our attention. And this is its significance as a sign of God's sovereign grace. In our Lord's conception by the Holy Spirit and birth of the virgin Mary, we are given a wonderful sign of the free grace and power of God.

No believer has to reflect long upon the birth of the Lord Jesus Christ of the virgin Mary in order to realize that this is a *miracle* in the strictest sense of the Word. It is an act of God's miraculous power and grace for which there is no "natural" explanation. It is an act that not only surpasses the possibilities of ordinary human conception, but it also transcends them utterly. There is only one thing to which it can be compared — and that

---

[17]*Ecumenical Creeds and Reformed Confessions*, p. 20.

[18]At various times in the history of the church, our Lord's conception by the Holy Spirit and birth of the virgin Mary have been wrongly associated with an unbiblical view of marriage and the transmission of original sin. In this view, the act of human generation implies sin and thus Christ's sinlessness required that He be born of a virgin. This view is also related to the Roman Catholic doctrine of the "immaculate conception" of the virgin Mary. Unless she was herself without inherited sin through the act of conception, she could not give birth to a sinless Savior. John Calvin aptly comments on this view in his *Institutes* (II.xiii.4): "For we make Christ free of all stain not just because he was begotten of his mother without copulation with man, but because he was sanctified by the Spirit that the generation might be pure and undefiled as would have been true before Adam's fall."

is God's work of creation in which He called into existence things that were not through His powerful Word. The work of the Spirit in the conception of the Lord Jesus Christ and his birth of the virgin Mary is, judged by the standard of the ordinary means of conception and birth, utterly impossible!

Interestingly, this is confirmed by the angel when he says to Mary in the context of the announcement of Christ's birth, "For nothing will be impossible with God" (Luke 1:37). Consequently, Mary, knowing the power and the grace of God's Word, replies, "... be it done to me according to your word" (v. 38).

We are given, therefore, in the birth of our Lord, a sign of God's free and sovereign initiative in the provision of redemption. We may say of Christ's birth what may be said of every believer's new birth, that He was "born not of blood, nor of the will of the flesh, nor of the will of man, but of God" (John 1:13). Like God's initiative in our new birth, the initiative of the Spirit in our Lord's conception reminds us that from first to last and in every particular our salvation is God's doing! Nowhere are we required to humble ourselves before the sovereign working of God's grace more than in the face of this miracle of God's grace in Christ's birth.[19]

Thus, in this miracle of Christ's birth we have a reminder of the miracle of our own new birth by the Spirit. Though we must beware the temptation to detract from the uniqueness of the Spirit's work in the conception and birth of Christ, His birth reminds us that the provision of salvation through Christ is an act exclusively of God's sovereign grace and power.

---

[19]It is interesting that theologians as different as Herman Hoeksema and Karl Barth have emphasized this. Unfortunately, Barth undermines his emphasis upon the virgin birth as a "sign" of God's sovereign grace by hesitating to insist upon it as a simple historical fact or occurrence. Hoeksema, in his *Reformed Dogmatics* (Grand Rapids, MI: Reformed Free Publishing, 1966), p. 352, says it well: "...certain it is that God purposely creates the sign of the virgin birth to make it known unto us that Jesus Christ's coming into the flesh is His act exclusively, and that Christ is born not by the will of man, but by the conception of the Holy Ghost."

The place of the virgin Mary

It would not be appropriate to conclude our consideration of this article in the Creed without commenting upon the legitimate place which it ascribes to the virgin Mary. This is particularly important in view of the wrongful place that many have and continue to ascribe to her in their understanding of the Christian faith.

The first comment here is a negative one. There is no place granted to Mary in this article of the Creed or in the Scriptures which elevates her to a position alongside of Christ. Because of her unique role in serving through God's grace as an instrument to give birth to the Savior, however, some have ascribed to Mary the title of "co-mediatrix" or contributor to Christ's saving work. Appeal is then made to the Bible's declaration of her blessedness as the "mother of our Lord" (Luke 1:42,48).

In the development of a Mariology in the Roman Catholic Church, for example, this ascription to Mary of a role *alongside* of Christ in the accomplishment of redemption is expressed in the teachings of her "Immaculate Conception" and "Bodily Assumption." The "Immaculate Conception" of Mary, first set forth as official dogma by the church in 1854, means that she as well as Christ was born without the stain of original sin. Her "Bodily Assumption," first set forth as official dogma by the church in 1950, means that her body was raised from the grave shortly after her death and reunited with her soul, whereupon she was assumed into heaven to be with her Son the "Queen of heaven." Clearly, in both of these teachings, as well as in the teaching that Mary was "perpetually a virgin," we have the development of a view of Mary's person and contribution to the accomplishment of salvation which takes from Christ what belongs to Him alone! These teachings do not enjoy any biblical support but represent a tendency to ascribe to Christ's human mother a role in the history of redemption which is antithetical to the church's confession concerning the person and work of Jesus Christ.[20]

---

[20] The title often ascribed to Mary, "mother of God," though it has come to be associated with an unwarranted emphasis upon her virtue and work, was originally used by

The second comment is a positive one. In our repudiation of any view of Mary's place in the gospel record which compromises the sole sufficiency and exclusive prerogative of Christ as Savior, we must not fall prey to an unbiblical belittling of Mary's place in the birth of Christ. Certainly, it was and remains a great favor which God has given her to be the one who bore in her womb this child who was the incarnate Son of God! Though this was entirely a gift of His grace and in no respect something which she deserved or merited, it was a favor shown to and received by her for which we may and must continue to call her "blessed."

Moreover, we should not overlook the manner in which Mary herself is said in the Scriptures to have responded to this gift of God's grace and expression of His power. In her response to the Word of God concerning the child to be born, expressing as it did the miracle of God's gracious provision of this child who would be called the Son of God, she is said to have subscribed in simple faith to its truth. She believed God! And what an amazing thing it was, as we have seen, in which she believed! Certainly, we must see in this a "type" of that obedience of faith to which all believers are called in their response to the Word of God. We too must echo the words of Elizabeth, "Blessed is she who believed that there would be a fulfillment of what had been spoken to her by the Lord" (Luke 1:45).

And so we come full circle. Just as Mary believed this Word of God and sang God's praises at the announcement of the Savior's birth, so may we. In the face of so much unbelief and disobedience to the Word of God, we are free to believe and confess with great joy and humble amazement that our Lord was "conceived by the Holy Spirit, born of the virgin Mary."

Mary's song of faith belongs to the whole church, when she says, "My soul exalts the Lord, and my spirit has rejoiced in God my Savior.... He has given help to Israel his servant, in remem-

---

the church in her confession (Chalcedon, 451 A.D.) to express the *unity* of Christ's person in two natures, divine and human. Therefore, when the creed spoke of Mary as "mother of God," it meant to affirm that the child born from her womb was none other than the eternal Son of God become incarnate. It did not mean to teach what is in fact impossible — that Mary was, in respect to His divine nature, the mother of the eternal Son.

brance of His mercy, as He spoke to our fathers, to Abraham and his offspring forever" (Luke 1:46,54-55).

Recommended reading:

J. Gresham Machen. *The Virgin Birth of Christ.* New York: Harper & Brothers, 1930.

Questions for Discussion

1. Where in the Bible is the virgin birth of Jesus Christ taught? How would you respond to someone who said, "because there is not an account of the virgin birth in every gospel, this is probably a legend created by the early church"?

2. The Presbyterian theologian, John Murray, has suggested that we speak of the "virgin conception" rather than the "virgin birth" of Christ. Why would he make this suggestion?

3. How is the virgin birth of Christ related to His saving work as our Mediator?

4. How would you respond to someone who argued that the doctrine of the virgin birth is not an essential doctrine of the Christian faith?

5. The Roman Catholic church teaches the perpetual virginity, the immaculate conception and the bodily assumption of the virgin Mary. Explain the meaning of these teachings. How would you show from the Scriptures that they are not biblical?

6. May or should believers today call Mary the "mother of God"? Give one possible legitimate use of this language.

CHAPTER FIVE

"SUFFERED UNDER PONTIUS PILATE, WAS CRUCIFIED, DEAD, AND BURIED"

"For while we were still helpless, at the right time Christ died for the ungodly. For one will hardly die for a righteous man; though perhaps for the good man someone would dare even to die. But God demonstrates His own love toward us, in that while we were yet sinners, Christ died for us. Much more then, having now been justified by His blood, we shall be saved from the wrath of God through Him." Romans 5:6-9

"For God so loved the world, that He gave His only begotten Son." John 3:16

"He suffered under Pontius Pilate" — these words in the Apostles' Creed, words which summarize the whole of Christ's life, are so brief and focused exclusively upon suffering that they have often been criticized. What of the remainder of Christ's life, His "earthly ministry" as we often term it? What of His teaching which was so unique and powerful that it provoked the amazement of the crowds who observed that He taught as having authority and not as their scribes (Matt. 7:28-29)? What of His many mighty works of healing? Surely this summary of the life's work of our Lord Jesus Christ is too brief and ignores important aspects of what He has done for our salvation.

We have to be careful here. After all, the Creed is only a summary and in a summary you always want to say what must be

50

said and what expresses the central thing. It should not surprise us, therefore, when the Creed passes over in silence a number of aspects of Christ's work. Nor should this mislead us into thinking that the Creed were saying these aspects are of no consequence to us and Christ's saving work. We should not be tempted by this to make the mistake of some — including no less than Calvin himself in his Catechism! — who say that the events preceding Christ's passion do not belong to "the substance of our redemption."

What we must see is that this description of Christ's work, "He suffered under Pontius Pilate," properly recounts not only His saving work at the end of the His life but His saving work throughout the whole course of His life. His life was, as the Heidelberg Catechism so well notes, a life of suffering from beginning to end. Answering the question as to the meaning of the word, "suffered," the Catechism says, "That during his whole life on earth, but especially at the end, Christ sustained in body and soul the anger of God against the sin of the whole human race" (Lord's Day 15).[21]

These words of the Creed — "He suffered under Pontius Pilate, was crucified, dead and buried" — remind us that all of His saving work was epitomized in His suffering under Pontius Pilate. In these words the centerpiece of the story of our Lord's saving work is described. And we are reminded that this is a glorious, yet sobering, story, one whose depths we can only begin to plumb as we stammer to speak and confess!

"He suffered"

If these words summarize the whole of Christ's life and saving work for us, we must be clear about the nature and purpose of this work. To put it more precisely, we have to ask — what did He suffer and why did He suffer?

This is especially important today, because much is being written and said about our "participation" in the sufferings of Christ. In a world where suffering is a commonplace and where

---

[21]*Ecumenical Creeds and Reformed Confessions*, p. 21.

the forms of suffering are so many and oftentimes so terrible, there is an understandable tendency to relate directly these forms of suffering to Christ's suffering. There is a tendency to look for what these forms of suffering have in common with the suffering of Christ. Some even speak of Christ's suffering *in* and *with* the suffering of the impoverished, the homeless, the marginalized, the oppressed. And so they speak, for example, of Christ's suffering with the pain and suffering of the Jewish people during the holocaust or with the poor of the earth today.[22]

In this search for the common bond between Christ's suffering and the suffering so pervasive in this sin-cursed world in which we live, there is a failure to recognize the *utter uniqueness* of the suffering of our Lord Jesus Christ. His suffering is unique not only because of the uniqueness of His person as the eternal Son who became man in the incarnation, the God-man; but it is also unique in that it was a suffering of the wrath and displeasure of God with us on account of our sin. In the suffering of our Lord Jesus Christ, we witness the incomparable and marvelous reality of God in the person of the Son bearing that condemnation for sin that was our deserving.

When we confess that our Lord suffered during the whole course of His life but especially at the end, we confess that in His suffering He "sustained in body and soul the anger of God against the sin of the whole human race." Admittedly, this is an increasingly unpopular emphasis today, and one which is sadly denied even by some who confess the words of the Creed. There is little enthusiasm or appreciation for the truth that our Lord Jesus Christ suffered as our substitute the wrath and displeasure of God because of our sin.

But it is impossible to avoid the teaching of Scripture that it was precisely this which characterized and distinguished the suffering of our Lord. The words of Isaiah 53 form the background to the New Testament accounts of our Lord's suffering: "Surely our griefs He Himself bore, and our sorrows He carried;

[22]It is remarkable that even so capable and sound an interpreter of the biblical teaching about Christ's suffering, John R. Stott, commits this error in his *The Cross of Christ* (Downer's Grove, IL: Intervarsity Press, 1986), pp. 329-337.

yet we ourselves esteemed Him stricken, smitten of God, and afflicted. But He was pierced through for our transgressions, He was crushed for our iniquities" (vv. 4-5). There is no other explanation for the "darkness" that fell upon the land from the sixth to the ninth hour during His crucifixion, at the end of which He cried out — "My God, My God, why hast Thou forsaken Me?" (Matt. 27:45-46). This darkness speaks of God's judgment, the withdrawal of His favor and blessing, the excommunication of the sinner from His presence. Similarly, the apostle Paul says that He was "delivered up because of our transgression, and was raised because of our justification" (Rom. 4:25). God "made Him who knew no sin to be sin on our behalf, that we might become the righteousness of God in Him" (2 Cor. 5:21).

In these and many other passages, we are taught that Christ suffered the holy displeasure of God in our place. In a way that is unspeakably glorious, the Father provided us a demonstration of His own love in giving His Son in our place as the One who would bear our sin's deserving and satisfy God's justice. Thus, in the substitutionary suffering of our Lord Jesus Christ, God also provided us a demonstration of His justice "that He might be just and the justifier of the one who has faith in Jesus" (Rom. 3:25-26). In our Lord's suffering we see the perfect harmony, and not the dissonance which many imagine, between God's love and justice.

"Under Pontius Pilate"

One remarkable feature of the Creed's summary of Christ's suffering is the reference to "Pontius Pilate." The inclusion of the name of Pontius Pilate in the Creed has often been the occasion for puzzlement and surprise in the church. By what right does this political opportunist and instrument through whom our Lord was crucified obtain a place in this summary of the church's faith? In a Creed whose words are few and whose focus is upon that which must be said, why must we include this reference to Pontius Pilate? This question was strikingly underscored by the English novelist, Dorothy L. Sayers, in a play written for the English radio, "The Man Born to be King," when she portrays Procla, the wife of Pilate, hearing in a dream the question being raised throughout subsequent centuries, "'Suffered under Pontius Pilate,' how comes this Pontius Pilate into the Creed?"

Two things come to mind immediately in response to this question.

First, we are reminded that our confession deals with the reality of our Lord's suffering. None of this is a fantasy of our imagination, or merely a symbol of universal suffering. It is the stuff of which history, the history in which you and I find our life and home, is made. The suffering of our Lord can be defined in terms of its time and place, and the circumstances which surrounded and led up to it. Its occurrence cannot be denied, despite the foolishness of some who today would deny it. Christ's suffering took place "under Pontius Pilate," that is, in the time and place, with all of the accompanying circumstances which are recounted in the gospel records.[23]

And second, we see the wisdom and hand of the Father in the suffering of our Lord. Through Pontius Pilate, whose authority and power was not His own but "from God," the innocence of our Savior was declared (John 19:4,11). His perfect sinlessness and the false charges brought against Him were exposed through Pilate's declaration of His guiltlessness. And thereby we are reminded that He suffered, not for His own sins but for the sins of His people. We are reminded that He was condemned, though innocent, on our behalf and in our stead, so that we who are guilty before God might be acquitted. "For Christ also died for sins once for all, the just for the unjust, in order that He might bring us to God" (2 Pet. 3:18).

This reveals as well the "why" of our Lord's suffering. Often we hear the question asked — why did the eternal Son become man? But this question needs to be rephrased and sharpened in

---

[23]Some of my readers may have had the misfortune of hearing of the "Jesus Seminar." This is a group of biblical "scholars" who are attempting to determine what is historical and what is fictional in the New Testament accounts of the life and ministry of Jesus Christ. One of their "findings" is that the New Testament's teaching that Jesus suffered and died as an atonement for sin is a later theological interpretation of Jesus' life. Against this folly, the Creed simply reminds us in the words, "suffered under Pontius Pilate," that all of this has to do with *real history*, with the *event* of Christ's saving work upon the cross.

the form — why did the eternal Son become man in order to suffer and die?

Here our answer may be brief. He did this for us and for our salvation! He did this in order that He might be the Savior of those who belong to Him and whom the Father would give Him. Because He suffered the Father's displeasure with us in our sin, because He endured the penalty of our sin, because He offered Himself in our place — we may believe that He earned for us our acceptance with God. As the Heidelberg Catechism again expresses it, "This he did in order that, by His suffering as the only atoning sacrifice, He might set us free, body and soul, from eternal condemnation, and gain for us God's grace, righteousness, and eternal life."[24]

"Was Crucified, Dead and Buried"

All of this is only reinforced and accentuated by the added words, "was crucified, dead and buried."

It is of special importance to notice that our Lord who suffered under Pontius Pilate was "crucified." In the children's catechism my wife and I have used in our home to instruct our children, the question is asked — "What kind of death did Christ die?" The answer which our children are taught to give is, "The painful and shameful death of the cross."

But those words don't begin — how could words be found to express it? — to express the awful reality of crucifixion. For the cross, though it is that in which as believers we glory (Gal. 6:14) and which as preachers we must preach (1 Cor. 2:2), is an emblem of suffering and shame. It is a sign of being under the curse of God! It means to be in the place of abandonment and forsaken-ness, to be excommunicated from every token and expression of God's favor and blessing. As the apostle Peter so powerfully expresses it, "He Himself bore our sins in His body on the cross" (1 Pet. 2:24). Or as the apostle Paul explicitly asserts, "Christ redeemed us from the curse of the Law, having become a curse

---

[24]*Ecumenical Creeds and Reformed Confessions*, p. 21.

for us — for it is written, 'Cursed is everyone who hangs upon a tree'" (Gal. 3:13).

We need to be careful here too, for we are not to think that the eternal Father of our Lord Jesus Christ ever ceased to love the Son, even in this event of His being abandoned upon the cross as our sin-bearer. Never did the Father love Him more, though (for our sakes!) He withdrew from Him every token of His favor and "bruised Him for our iniquities."

Who can comprehend this? Who can reflect upon it without fear and trembling? We must beware the arrogance of trying to comprehend it fully or to plumb the depths of it. As the Dutch theologian Klaas Schilder once remarked, no one can comprehend the crucifixion of Christ unless they have been in hell! And they could not even understand it then, for they would not have been in hell the way Christ was who, as the eternal and perfectly holy Son, merited only the fullness of the Father's love and favor. It is best to fall silent. Certainly we should guard ourselves against that morbid fascination which some display when they try to describe in explicit and complete detail the manner in which our Lord may have been crucified, or when they endeavor to enter into the experience of His crucifixion for themselves.

But then there are finally added the simple, yet important, words, "dead and buried."

These words are added with good reason. They actually provide a summary and conclusion of the words preceding. For our Lord's suffering under Pontius Pilate, His being crucified, was an obedience unto death, even the death of the cross. Not one thing was left undone. The curse of sin is death. For Christ to suffer this curse required that He suffer it fully and completely.

This is also the good news of our confession that our Lord, who suffered the condemnation due us in His suffering and crucifixion, who bore the curse which was rightfully due the sinner in the sinner's place — that He was dead and buried. His body was laid lifeless in the grave, a corpse requiring to be wrapped in linen cloth and prepared with spices and perfumes (Luke 24:53ff.). This tells us that He did it! His burial confirms that He finished it! And for us!

This means everything for us, especially when we think "ahead" as we must to the next words of our confession — "He arose again on the third day." Because it means that death, death as God's judgment and curse upon our sinful selves and lives, has been put to death in the death of Christ. We need no longer fear it. We need no longer live as though it possessed any final power over us. We no longer have to resort to the kind of morbid humor evident in the quip of the movie director and actor, Woody Allen, when he says, "I am not afraid of my death; I just do not want to be there when it happens!" When as believers we stand at the gravesite of a fellow believer, the light of the gospel overpowers the shadow of death. Christ has gone before us. He entered into the domain of death. Christ was "dead and buried." But He is alive and so are we, because the wages of sin have been paid and the victory has been won.[25]

Conclusion

However difficult it may be for us to comprehend and to fathom the confession we make about the suffering and death of our Savior, it remains the heart of our confession concerning His saving work.

There are two concluding comments that need to be made here, in addition to those we have already noted as we have considered this article in the Creed.

The first has to do with what this tells us about our sin and Christ's work of atonement for sin. It is impossible to confess with the Creed the suffering and death of Christ upon the cross without being struck by God's estimate of sin. There is no escaping the conclusion that the wages of sin are death, and that the just penalty for anyone who sins against the majesty and

---

[25]It is tragic that in some Reformed churches which should be *proclaiming* the Word of Christ's victory over sin and death in His cross and resurrection, the old Catholic and Medieval practice of *re-enacting* the crucifixion of the Lord in the "Tenebrae" service and by other means has been recently introduced. We cannot, however, re-enact our Lord's suffering. To attempt to do so is wrong and futile. We can (and may!) only *celebrate* through the Word preached and the sacrament administered the life obtained for us through Christ's work done for us *once for all* upon the cross.

holiness of God, is eternal death. This is a highly unpopular conclusion, to be sure, but it is inescapable. No one can begin to understand Christ's saving work by way of His suffering and death upon the cross without gaining a proper estimate of the ugliness and consequence of sin. This is also the reason why the cross remains a stumbling block, an occasion of offense, to anyone who does not want to reckon honestly with the reality and consequence of His own sin against God. It is also the reason those who endeavor to avoid the preaching of the cross do so invariably because they want to avoid the preaching of sin and its consequence.

The second has to do with what this tells us about God's love and justice. Though these are often said to be in contradiction or in tension with each other, the cross reveals both the love and the justice of God. God is in Christ *loving in His justice and just in His loving*. It reminds us that God has in love provided in His Son a substitute to carry our sin and pay its penalty. It also reminds us that God has done this in perfect conformity with His own justice.

This stands in marked contrast to the sentimentalizing of God's love which is so prevalent today. The "god" whom many profess is someone who winks at sin, who accommodates the sinner in his sin, and who could not be so perfectly just as to require satisfaction for sin. The suffering and cross of Christ testify to us that God in His justice could only receive us into His favor and fellowship by way of providing this atonement for sin. Those who deny, therefore, the substitutionary work of our Lord in satisfying God's justice, remove not a dispensable "theory" of the atonement, but the revelation of God's love and justice — of Himself! — in that work.

Those who make this confession, accordingly, should anticipate hostility and rejection in the world from those who stumble at the cross. In this way the believer "participates" in the suffering of Christ, not as one who adds to a suffering which is otherwise incomplete and insufficient, but as one who suffers on account of and for the sake of this confession of the suffering Christ. "For indeed Jews ask for signs, and Greeks search for wisdom; but we preach Christ crucified, to Jews a stumbling block, and to Gentiles foolishness, but to those who are the called, both Jews and

Greeks, Christ the power of God and the wisdom of God" (1 Cor. 2:22-23).

Recommended reading:

Berkouwer, Gerrit C. *The Work of Christ.* Grand Rapids, MI: Eerdmans, 1965.

Letham, Robert. *The Work of Christ.* Downer's Grove, IL: Intervarsity, 1993.

Murray, John. *Redemption Accomplished and Applied.* Grand Rapids, MI: Eerdmans, 1955.

Stott, John R. *The Cross of Christ.* Downer's Grove, IL: Intervarsity, 1986.

Questions for Discussion

1. What was unique about the suffering of Jesus Christ?

2. Why do we speak of the "substitutionary" atonement of Jesus Christ? What does this tell us about the "extent" of Christ's atoning work (for whom did He die)?

3. In what way may we speak of a "participation" in the suffering of Christ (compare Col. 1:24)?

4. Explain why the Apostles' Creed adds the words, "under Pontius Pilate." Consider the account in John 19:1-15 in your answer.

5. What was the importance of Christ's death being a death by crucifixion? Consider 1 Peter 2:24, Galatians 3:13, and Philippians 2:8, in your answer.

6. How are believers comforted by the death and burial of Jesus Christ?

7. How does the cross of Christ reveal to us the mercy and the justice of God?

8. Why is it wrong to attempt to remember Christ's suffering by means of a worship service which re-enacts His suffering (e.g. the *Tenebrae*)?

CHAPTER SIX

"HE DESCENDED INTO HELL"

"Now from the sixth hour darkness fell upon all the land until the ninth hour. And about the ninth hour Jesus cried out with a loud voice, saying, 'Eli, Eli, lama sabachthani?' that is, 'My God, My God, why hast Thou forsaken Me?'"
Matthew 27:45-46

In the secular western world in which you and I live, the language of many people betrays a faint echo of a Christian past but little more. Oftentimes biblical words and phrases are employed, but they have a hollow ring. They have been emptied of their biblical content and significance. When as Christian believers we "overhear" the language of the playground or of the television "fare" that comes into our homes, we are often dismayed by this contrast between the language of faith and the language of the world.

Nowhere is this more strikingly evident than in the use today of the word "hell." This is a word which is deeply rooted in the biblical view of sin and its consequence in the way of God's judgment upon the sinner. It is a word which gives poignant expression to the depth dimension of our Lord's suffering on behalf of His people. Our Lord — whom we confess "suffered under Pontius Pilate, was crucified, dead and buried" — "descended into hell." This declares to us something of what He did to accomplish our salvation — He suffered hell in our place and on our behalf. Here we speak in the language of faith, echoing the teaching of God's Word about the saving work of our Lord Jesus Christ.

But how different is the language of the world! "Hell" has become a common vulgarity. It is used to impress others with the bravado or the courage of the one who speaks. Frequently, it is tossed out in the form of a curse spoken against a fellow human being — lightly, as though to consign a person to hell were a small thing! Or it is used like salt and pepper to sprinkle one's conversation, to give it bite and taste! But in all of this the biblical meaning of "hell" has been lost to many.

The Apostles' Creed, by its inclusion of this article, reminds us that "hell" is real. The reality of hell belongs to our confession concerning what our Lord suffered. In our consideration of the meaning of this article, we will begin by considering two traditional views which are not supported by the Scriptures. Then, we will give a biblical, Reformed interpretation of our Lord's descent into hell, followed by a comment on its significance for us.

Two traditional views

Before explaining the historic Reformed understanding of this article in the Creed, it is necessary that we consider two traditional views of Christ's descent into hell. Because this article follows upon the description of a series of events in sequence — "suffered under Pontius Pilate, was crucified, dead and buried" — and comes immediately before the confession of our Lord's resurrection from the dead, the oldest understanding has taken it to refer to a literal descent of our Lord to the place of the dead, hell or "hades," which occurred after His death and before His resurrection on the third day. This literal understanding of our Lord's descent into hell has taken two forms in traditional Roman Catholicism and Lutheranism.[26]

---

[26]This article was not included in the earliest forms of the Apostle's Creed. It was only first included in the Aquileian form of the Creed in 390 A.D. (*descendit ad inferna*). It will be evident from the discussion of the two traditional views of this article in Roman Catholicism and Lutheranism that the oldest interpretation has been to take this as referring to a local and literal descent into hell, the place of the dead, after Christ's death upon the cross.

In the traditional Roman Catholic understanding, it is said that Christ, after his death, went to the *Limbus patrum*, the "place of the Fathers," where the Old Testament saints were awaiting the revelation and application of Christ's redemption. When the Creed speaks of Christ's descent into "hell," it refers to a literal going to this place of the dead, this interim location of the Old Testament believers who looked forward to the coming of Christ. Because Christ's great work of atonement was completed, He visited this *Limbus patrum* in order to grant these Old Testament believers a share in His saving work. By His death, Christ destroyed the power of sin and death and opened the gate of Paradise. By His descent into hell, He granted these believers a share in His victory. The "hell" into which Christ descended, therefore, is not that place of provisional and anticipatory punishment to which the unbelieving and impenitent are consigned upon death (compare Luke 16:19,31). It is simply that intermediate state of the Old Testament believer, the place of the believing dead, which precedes their entrance through Christ's atoning work into Paradise.

The problem with this position is that it has simply no biblical support. Sometimes appeal is made to the words of the apostle Peter at Pentecost, quoting from Psalm 16:8-10:

> And so, because he was a prophet [that is, David in Psalm 16], and knew that God had sworn to him with an oath to seat one of his descendants upon his throne, he looked ahead and spoke of the resurrection of the Christ, that "He was neither abandoned to hades, nor did his flesh suffer decay." (Acts 2:30-31)

But this passage cites two statements in the Psalm which parallel each other and say the same thing in two different ways — Christ would not be left by God to the power of death! Both phrases, "He was neither abandoned to hades" and "nor did His flesh suffer decay," have this identical meaning. They do not speak of a descent into the *Limbus patrum* for the purpose of releasing the Old Testament saints and granting them entry into heaven.

The other text frequently appealed to in support of this position is found in 1 Peter 3:18-20:

> For Christ also died for sins once for all, the just for the unjust, in order that He might bring us to God, having been put to death in the flesh, but made alive in the Spirit; in which also He went and made proclamation to the spirits now in prison, who once were disobedient, when the patience of God kept waiting in the days of Noah ....

However, this passage, though it is difficult to interpret, says nothing that supports the historic Roman Catholic understanding of Christ's descent into hell. It refers, not to a literal descent into hell, but to a proclaiming work of Christ by means of the life-giving Spirit to the "spirits in prison." These "spirits in prison," moreover, are not Old Testament saints at all. They are the fallen angels who were disobedient in the days of Noah and who were cast into this prison or place of judgment by God (compare 2 Peter 2:4,5; Jude 6; Gen. 6:1-4). Nowhere in the Scriptures do we find the word "spirits" used, as it is here, alone and without qualification, to designate believers, whether the Old Testament fathers or New Testament believers.[27]

The other view, one which has a secure place in traditional Lutheran teaching, takes this article to refer to the "first step" of Christ's exaltation in which He went into the underworld, the place of the dead, to reveal and consummate His victory over Satan and the powers of darkness. This view understands Christ's preaching as a "heralding" or "declaring" to disobedient and

---

[27]One other passage often cited, and one which we will briefly consider in conjunction with the traditional view of Lutheranism, is 1 Peter 4:4-6: "And in all this, they are surprised that you do not run with them into the same excess of dissipation, and they malign you; but they shall give account to Him who is ready to judge the living and the dead. For the gospel has for this purpose been preached even to those who are dead, that though they are judged in the flesh as men, they may live in the spirit according to the will of God." This passage, however, does not provide any real support for the idea of a literal descent by Christ into the place of the dead to preach the gospel or announce His victory. Christ is not said in this passage to be the one who preaches this gospel to the dead (no subject is expressly mentioned for this preaching). Nor is there any reason to believe that the "dead" referred to in this passage were not alive when the gospel was preached to them.

imprisoned spirits in hell or hades, the event of His victory over sin and death. Though there is a divergence within historic Lutheranism as to whether this preaching occurred before or after the resurrection, it is never understand to be a preaching to the Old Testament saints as a prelude to their reception into heaven with Christ. It is rather a pronouncing of Christ's victory and the sentence of condemnation that falls upon the unbelieving and disobedient spirits in hell.

This view is certainly preferable to that of historic Roman Catholicism. It fits better with the reference in 1 Peter 3:18-20 to a preaching to the spirits who once were disobedient in the days of Noah. Nevertheless, there is insufficient biblical evidence to authorize our acceptance of it as a proper view of this article in the Creed. Not only does 1 Peter 3:18-20 refer to a preaching authored by the life-giving Spirit who imparted life to Christ (and not to Christ Himself preaching); but it also refers to a preaching directed particularly to spirits who were disobedient in the days of Noah, not to spirits generally who were imprisoned for their disobedience. Additionally, the only other reference in Scripture to a preaching to "those who are dead" (1 Peter 4:4-6) refers to a preaching of the gospel to the unbelieving. The preaching referred to in this passage is not directed to the spirits in prison or hell. Presumably, it describes the preaching of the gospel by a minister of the Word and not exclusively the preaching of Christ Himself.

Because neither of these traditional, literal understandings of Christ's descent into hell has biblical support, therefore, we must turn to consider the alternative, Reformed view.

The Reformed view

In the Reformed tradition, this article of the Creed has been interpreted metaphorically as a description, not of one event in a sequence of events which describe successive moments in Christ's saving work, but of the nature and depth of what He suffered for us in His work of atonement.[28] Our Lord Jesus Christ, in all that suffered under Pontius Pilate, in His being crucified, in His death and burial, underwent the torment and penalty of God-forsaken-ness in the place and on behalf of His people.

Thus, we are not to understand the confession of our Lord's descent into hell as though it were describing a literal descent, subsequent to His death and burial, to hell or hades as the place of the dead. Rather, we are to understand this article as express-ing the epitome of all of our Lord's suffering in His atoning work as our substitute. The article, "He descended into hell," does not so much add something to the other articles in their description of our Lord's suffering, crucifixion and death, as it expresses the heart of what He suffered — He was abandoned and forsaken by the Father. He suffered that God-forsakenness which was our due in our place.

This view of our Lord's descent into hell expresses powerfully the biblical understanding of our Lord's suffering. When we read, for example, in Matthew's gospel that "darkness fell over all the earth" from the sixth to the ninth hour in the circumstance of our Lord's crucifixion, we are taught that He was cast into the "outer darkness" of the Father's disfavor and wrath upon the sinner in whose place He stood. And so we are given to understand, though we shall never be able to comprehend it, why it was that He cried out at the end of the ninth hour, "My God, My God, why hast Thou forsaken me?" Think of it — the eternal Son of the Father, the Son whom the Father always loved with a perfect love, abandoned and cut off from any token of the Father's favor in our place!

But it is not only the biblical description of Christ's suffering that has led the Reformed churches to understand His descent into hell in this fashion. It is also the biblical teaching that Christ finished this suffering upon the cross. How else are we to understand His confident declaration to one of the criminals crucified with Him, "Truly I say to you, today you shall be with Me

---

[28]Actually, it is something of an overstatement to call this *the* Reformed view. In the Westminster Larger Catechism, Q. & A. 50, the descent into hell is simply equated with Christ's death and burial.

in Paradise" (Luke 23:43)? Or, how are we to understand His words from the cross, "[I]t is finished" (John 19:30) and "Father, into Thy hands I commit My spirit" (Luke 23:46)? The notion of a literal descent into hell, subsequent to His death and burial, is inconsistent with what these passages affirm. Christ, having suffered the penalty of sin, having suffered the agony of hellish forsakenness and abandonment under the curse of God against the sinner, committed Himself to His Father in the confidence of a work finished and Paradise gained!

For our warning and comfort

There have been some in the history of the church, even in Reformed churches, who have argued that this article should be deleted from the Creed, simply because it is subject to misunderstanding or even, as we have seen, unbiblical interpretation. It must be admitted, of course, that no article in the church's Creed is exempt from "critical" scrutiny by the standard of the written Word. This holds true as well for this article. We cannot say, therefore, that in principle it would be impossible and invariably wrong to remove it.

Yet, it would constitute a great loss were this article removed from the Creed solely because it has so often been understood in an unbiblical way. It would be a loss because, as the Reformed churches have understood it, this article expresses an (if not, *the*) essential dimension of our Lord's suffering and atoning work. This article powerfully interprets the articles which precede it, since it expresses the reality of what our Lord suffered in an unmistakable and emphatic way. Because it is biblical in what affirms, and because it expresses this central thing in our Lord's suffering on our behalf, we should retain it.[29]

---

[29]That an article in the church's creed or confession has been commonly understood in an unbiblical way is not itself sufficient reason to have it removed. The most important question in respect to any article in the creed is: does it agree with and express some aspect of biblical teaching? Certainly, this article does express an important aspect of the work of Christ — not His literal descent into hell after His death, but a suffering of the torment of hell on behalf of His people.

In the light of our discussion of the meaning of our Lord's descent into hell, there are two further observations that I would like to underscore.

First, to return to the place at which we began, this article reminds us that hell is real. Just as we noted in the previous article that the suffering and crucifixion of our Lord reminds us of the gravity and consequence of sin, so here with our Lord's descent into hell we are taught that hell is what we sinners deserve! However unpalatable and even unacceptable this may be to our secular world, including some who are secular within the church, the biblical teaching that the sinner deserves to be abandoned by and delivered over to the eternal death of punishment in hell cannot be escaped. Anyone who confesses with biblical understanding the descent of Christ into hell must acknowledge this truth. The hell He endured was the hell I deserved at the hand of God!

This undergirds the biblical urgency of preaching the gospel of salvation through the atoning work of Jesus Christ. It explains why we must proclaim the gospel as the only way of escape from the consequences of sin. And it requires that those who preach the gospel bring not only the "good news" of God's provision in Christ for those who believe and repent, but also the "warning" of the awful consequence of unbelief and impenitence. No gospel preacher who knows the consequences of sin will fail urgently to call upon all to work out their salvation "with fear and trembling." By this measure, there are some today who preach a "gospel" which is not biblically authorized, for they refuse to speak of salvation from sin and its consequence through the atoning work of Christ, including His having descended into hell!

And second, this article is part of the believer's comfort. In the Heidelberg Catechism, the question asked concerning this article is, "Why does the Creed add: 'He descended into hell'?" The answer given captures well this comfort,"To assure me in times of personal crisis and temptation that Christ my Lord, by suffering unspeakable anguish, pain, and terror of soul, especially on the cross but also earlier, has delivered me from the anguish and torment of hell."[30]

Contrary to the flippant and sacrilegious way in which many today speak of "hell," Christians confess Christ "descended into hell." And in so doing, they confess not only the gravity of sin's consequence but also the great comfort which is theirs in Christ. Whatever I may suffer as God's child or undergo for the sake of Christ's name and kingdom, nothing is able to separate me from the love of God which is in Christ Jesus, my Lord.

How do I know this? How can I be sure of this? Only through this confession — "He descended into hell." "He who did not spare His own Son, but delivered Him up for us all, how will He not also with Him freely give us all things?" (Rom. 8:32).

Recommended reading:

Peterson, Robert A. *Hell on Trial: The Case for Eternal Punishment.* Phillipsburg, NJ: Presbyterian & Reformed, 1995.

Questions for Discussion

1. Summarize and evaluate the historic Roman Catholic understanding of Christ's descent into hell.

2. Summarize and evaluate the historic Lutheran understanding of Christ's descent into hell.

3. 1 Peter 3:18-20 and 1 Peter 4:4-6 are two disputed passages, often cited to support the teaching that Christ literally descended into hell after His death upon the cross. Based upon a reading and study of these passages, what do you understand them to teach?

4. What is the most common Reformed understanding of Christ's descent into hell? What biblical arguments can be offered to support this understanding?

---

[30]*Ecumenical Creeds and Reformed Confessions*, p. 22.

5. Since the article in the Creed regarding Christ's descent into hell has been so much disputed, do you believe it would be wise to remove it from the Creed, as many suggest today? Give reasons for your answer.

6. Some Reformed believers have suggested that the article, "He descended into hell," should be placed before the language, "was dead and buried," to protect against misunderstanding this descent in a literal way. Evaluate this suggestion.

7. How would your respond to the argument that it is dishonest to interpret an article in the Creed in a way that is biblical but contrary to the way in which it was originally understood?

8. What does this article in the Creed teach us about the doctrine of hell and eternal punishment?

CHAPTER SEVEN

"THE THIRD DAY HE ROSE AGAIN FROM THE DEAD"

"For if the dead are not raised, not even Christ has been raised; and if Christ has not been raised, your faith is worthless; you are still in your sins. Then those also who have fallen asleep in Christ have perished. If we have hoped in Christ in this life only, we are of all men most to be pitied. But now Christ has been raised from the dead, the first fruits of those who are asleep." 1 Corinthians 15:16-20

We live in a world which could easily lead one to despair. We read and hear constantly of developments and situations that are deeply disturbing and unsettling. The evening news program on the national networks, though it often only gives a fleeting glimpse of the news without adequate interpretation, bombards us with stories of refugees who have been driven from their homeland, terrorist activities in the Middle East, civil war and famine in Eritrea, the threat of civil war in South Africa, the slaughter of thousands of young student protestors in Tiannamen square in Beijing, etc. Wherever we look, we witness evidences of the pervasiveness of human sin and the curse which has been pronounced upon life in rebellion against God, a curse which includes the whole creation which is "groaning" in anticipation of the redemption of God's children (Rom. 8:18-22).

Now there are some whose answer to these evidences of human sin and death amounts to little more than a superficial denial of their reality. They market "positive" or "possibility" thinking as a way of salvation. The whole problem is one of perspective and attitude. If we see everything in a positive and hopeful light, and if we approach whatever obstacles we face with unstinting optimism, we will find life and blessedness. Robert Schuller has become famous by preaching this "gospel" of "possibility thinking. " In the face of whatever difficulties we encounter, we need only think possibilities and — voila! — we shall overcome them.

Our profession of faith as Christians is quite different, however. We believe that there is "good news" for this kind of world and fallen humanity only in the gospel of our Lord Jesus Christ. This gospel or "good news" is not that of a new perspective upon life but of a new reality in Christ brought about by God's grace and power. Jesus Christ is, as we have seen previously in our consideration of the Apostles' Creed, the only-begotten Son of God who became man in order to save us from our sins and from the death which marks our lives apart from God. Jesus Christ is the One who has come to us in order to restore us to fellowship and life with God. By His death upon the cross and His descent into hell, He has fully satisfied for all our sins and provided a way for us to be received again into God's favor.

The truth of this confession, however, hinges upon the article of the Creed that we are now to consider — "the third day he rose again from the dead." This article is absolutely crucial and indispensable to our confession of Christ's saving work. Without Christ's resurrection, nothing of what He did in His having been crucified or having descended into hell would be good news for us.

The resurrection of our Lord Jesus Christ on the third day, as an act of God's power and grace, therefore, is the bedrock upon which our confidence for salvation from sin and death is based. In our confession of Christ's resurrection we declare that Jesus Christ has risen as the *Victor* over sin and death. In the face of a world which still bears testimony to the remaining power of sin and death, we confess that there is salvation in Christ. As always our faith rests upon the reality of Jesus Christ — crucified and risen from the dead!

The reality of Christ's resurrection

Thomas Torrance, a well-known Scottish theologian, has written a little book entitled *Space, Time, and the Resurrection*. As the title suggests, Torrance argues in this book that the event of Christ's resurrection from the dead must be understood as an occurrence in space and time. It really happened! The same Jesus who was crucified, dead and buried, rose again on the third day. This is the reality we celebrate every Lord's Day on the first day of the week — "Christ is risen! He is risen indeed!"

Readers of the Scriptures will not be surprised by this argument of Torrance — it is so obvious! Believers throughout the centuries have always lived by an Easter faith. They have always confessed Christ, crucified and risen from the dead. We have an interesting confirmation of this in the Heidelberg Catechism which, in its treatment of this article in the Creed, simply presupposes the reality of Christ's resurrection and focuses all of its attention upon its "benefit" for the believer. The Catechism is not interested in a speculative "proof" for the resurrection or a detached treatment of its reality apart from its saving significance and meaning.

I mention Torrance's book, however, because it reminds us of how frequently many today call into question the reality of Christ's resurrection. So much so that for some it is a novel thing to confess the reality of the resurrection!

For a variety of reasons, there are many modern theologians and professed believers who waffle on the subject of the resurrection — did it happen or didn't it? A variety of clever reinterpretations have even been devised, each of which endeavors to affirm the significance of the resurrection for faith without actually affirming its event character. One popular reinterpretation, for example, suggests that the accounts of Christ's resurrection are the product of an "Easter faith" of the disciples. In this way, the disciples confessed the importance of Jesus for their lives and for others. The event of the resurrection, however, is only a "means" to express this importance. It is not to be taken literally, as something which occurred in the life of Jesus Christ. Though proponents of this view are no doubt sincere in their unbelief, their position is really no better than some who from the beginning concocted the story that the disciples had stolen Christ's body from the tomb and fabricated the story of His resurrection (compare Matt. 28:12-13)!

Though the Bible nowhere gives us a description of the resurrection — no one saw Christ arise — the account of the resurrection and Christ's resurrection appearances is found in all four gospels and in 1 Corinthians 15. Each of the gospel accounts concludes with the event of Christ's resurrection on the first day of the week. Together they constitute a fourfold witness to the fact that the tomb in which Christ's dead body was laid and to which the women and two of the disciples, Peter and John, came on the morning of the first day of the week — was empty (Matt. 28:1-15; Mark 16:1-13; Luke 24:1-12; John 20:1-18). The words of the angels in Luke 24:5-7, express well the heart of the matter, "Why do you seek the living One among the dead? He is not here, but He has risen. Remember how He spoke to you while He was still in Galilee, saying that the Son of Man must be delivered into the hands of sinful men, and be crucified, and the third day rise again."

The apostle Paul in 1 Corinthians 15:1-19 provides an extensive defense of the reality of Christ's resurrection. He not only begins by reminding his readers of the gospel which he was given to preach, the gospel of Christ's death and resurrection "according to the Scriptures," but he also cites those to whom Christ appeared after His resurrection as corroborating this gospel. He mentions, for example, the appearances of the resurrected Christ to Cephas and to the twelve, to more than five hundred brethren at one time, to James and to all the apostles, and last of all to himself. He testifies, therefore, with the other apostles as an eyewitness of the resurrection. He could say, in the words of the apostle John, "And he who has seen has borne witness, and his witness is true; and he knows that he is telling the truth, so that you also may believe" (John 19:35). Or in the words of the prologue to 1 John, "What was from the beginning, what we have heard, what we have seen with our eyes, what we beheld and our hands handled, concerning the Word of life" (v. 1; compare John 20:19-23).

Nothing could be more evident — the gospel declares that Christ, who was crucified, dead and buried, rose again on the third day!

The significance of Christ's resurrection

Though it may be necessary today to spend some time emphasizing the reality of Christ's resurrection from the dead on the third day, it is impossible to speak of its reality without immediately considering its significance. These are but two sides of one coin, since we cannot really know "what" happened when Christ rose on the third day unless we are biblically informed as to "what it means for us."

This is why those who argue solely for the "fact" of Christ's resurrection apart from a believing understanding of what it means are mistaken. Though it may be understandable that many believers today are tempted to "prove" the fact of the resurrection by appealing to the evidence which supports it, this approach will always be inadequate and self-defeating. For the resurrection of Christ on the third day is not simply a "bare fact," the "resuscitation of a corpse." What would it prove, were someone to convince us by the evidence that Christ rose on the third day? We need to be convinced in our confession of the resurrection of Christ "according to the Scriptures." Only those who confess the resurrection as a reality in terms of its Scriptural significance or meaning are properly submissive to the biblical testimony.

To understand something of the significance of Christ's resurrection, we need to recognize four distinct ways in which it benefits us.

The *first* benefit of the resurrection is that it establishes our right before God. The Heidelberg Catechism expresses it this way: "First, by his resurrection he has overcome death, so that he might make us share in the righteousness he won for us by his death."[31]

Why is the resurrection such a foundational and crucial aspect of the gospel? Why does everything finally rest upon the reality of our Lord's having been raised on the third day? This question

---

[31]*Ecumenical Creeds and Reformed Confessions*, p. 23.

can only be answered in the light of what we have already seen concerning His crucifixion and death. The resurrection of Christ unmistakably declares that His atoning sacrifice upon the cross was completed and acceptable to the Father. The resurrection demonstrates that the ransom has been paid and that the way has been opened for us into God's presence. His resurrection demonstrates to us that the death He died was the "death of death" for those who believe! Because Christ has been raised, we can be sure that we are no longer "in our sins," that is, we are no longer under the curse and judgment due us in our sins. By His crucifixion, death and burial, Christ paid the wages of sin for us. By His resurrection, the sufficiency of this payment is declared.

Consequently, the apostle Paul says in Romans 4:25 that Christ "was delivered up for our transgressions, and raised for our justification." This also underlies his words in Romans 5:8,10: "But God demonstrates His own love toward us, in that while we were yet sinners, Christ died for us. ... For if while we were enemies, we were reconciled to God through the death of the Son, much more, having been reconciled, we shall be saved by His life." If Christ's death means reconciliation for us through His satisfaction for our sins, how much more does His resurrection mean life for us! He lives as the One who has established our right before God. His resurrection is the ground upon which we have a right to stand before God: "Who will bring a charge against God's elect? God is the one who justifies; who is the one who condemns? Christ Jesus is He who died, yes, rather who was raised, who is at the right hand of God, who also intercedes for us" (Romans 8:3-34).

The *second* benefit of the resurrection is that it empowers us to live a new life. It is remarkable how often in the Scriptures the resurrection of Christ is joined, by virtue of our union with Christ, to our being restored in newness of life. When we are joined to Christ by the work of His Spirit and through faith, we die with Him to sin and we live with Him in newness of life!

Among the many Scriptural passages which speak of this second benefit of Christ's resurrection, I will cite only two. In an extensive passage on our union with Christ in His death and resurrection in Romans 6, the apostle Paul writes, "For the death that He died, He died to sin, once for all; but the life that He lives, He lives to God. Even so consider yourselves to be dead to sin, but alive to God in Christ Jesus" (vv. 10-11)." Similarly, in a passage in the same epistle, he argues that, "If the Spirit of Him who raised Christ from the dead dwells in you, He who raised Christ Jesus from the dead will also give life to your mortal bodies through His Spirit who indwells you" (Romans 8:11; compare Eph. 2:4-6; Col. 3:1-4; 2 Cor. 5:17).

What stands out in these passages, as well as others which express a similar theme, is that anyone who has been united with Christ through faith will inevitably share in His victory over sin and death. This share in His victory, moreover, is not simply a new *status* before God but a new *condition* of obedience. Those who are joined to the crucified and resurrected Christ are no longer under the dominion of sin. They are no longer, as they once were, slaves to sin, but rather they have become "slaves of righteousness" (Rom. 6:18).

The irony, of course, is that so many who "dust off" their faith as professing Christians around "Easter time" to celebrate Christ's resurrection, display little or nothing of this during the remainder of the year. They act as though one could profess the risen Christ without sharing in His resurrection life! But the gospel teaches that "anyone who is in Christ" is a "new creation; the old things passed away; behold, new things have come" (2 Cor. 5:17).

The *third* benefit of the resurrection is that it promises or guarantees our glorious resurrection. Much of the apostle Paul's argument in 1 Corinthians 15 consists of showing how, if believers are not raised from the dead, then Christ has not been raised. He can argue this way because the resurrection of Christ is joined to the resurrection of those who believe in Him in the same way as the "firstfruits" of a harvest are joined to the full harvest yet to come.

But now Christ has been raised from the dead, the first fruits of those who are asleep. For since by a man came death, by a man came also the resurrection of the dead. For as in Adam all die, so also in Christ all shall be made alive. But each in his own order: Christ the first fruits,

after that those who are Christ's at His coming. (1 Cor.
15:20-23)

For the Christian believer, therefore, the resurrection of Christ
is a pledge and guarantee of our future resurrection. We live as
believers confident that this "perishable" body must put on the
"imperishable," this "mortal will put on immortality" (1 Cor. 15:54).
Christ has by His resurrection won the victory over death, a
victory which He will not fail to share — as He shares all that
belongs to Himself — with His people (compare 1 Cor. 3:21-23).
This is our consolation when we face our own death, as well as
the death of fellow believers who have fallen asleep in Jesus.

But there is also in all of this a further benefit or aspect of the
significance of Christ's resurrection from the dead. The *fourth*
benefit of the resurrection is that it also confirms and attests the
person and work of our Lord. The apostle Paul says in Romans
1:3,4 that the Son "was born of a descendent of David according
to the flesh" and "was declared the Son of God with power by the
resurrection from the dead." Within the biblical setting of our
Lord's teaching and work, the resurrection authenticates His claim
to be the Son of God and validates His work as approved by the
Father.

Though unbelief will always err in denying His person and
work, the resurrection of Jesus Christ from the dead confirms for
the believer that He was indeed the One whom the Father sent
to save His people from their sins and that His work was in
accord with what the Scriptures declared concerning Him. For this
reason, when Thomas finally believed in the resurrected Lord,
confronted as He was with the living presence of the resurrected
Christ, He confessed "My Lord and my God" (John 20:28)! C.S.
Lewis once observed that we can only conclude from Christ's own
words and works that He was either mad or a deceiver or truly
the Son of God. The resurrection of Christ from the dead settles
this question for the believer. By virtue of His resurrection from
the dead on the third day, we know with a certainty that He is the
Christ, the Son of the living God.

Conclusion

In the midst of the world in which we live, the resurrection of Jesus Christ is always for the believer the great basis for hope. As the apostle Peter so remarkably expresses it, "Praise be to the God and Father of our Lord Jesus Christ! In His great mercy He has given us new birth into a living hope through the resurrection of Jesus Christ from the dead" (1 Pet. 1:3).

We have hope in the face of the remaining power and effects of sin because we know that the decisive victory has been accomplished. We live *anno domini*, in the "year of the Lord," in the time after His crucifixion and resurrection. Therefore, we rejoice even in the midst of our tribulation because we know our Savior lives — "Death no longer is the stronger, hell itself is captive led."

Oscar Cullmann, a New Testament scholar, once suggested that the resurrection of our Lord is to the final victory of God over sin, death, and the devil, what "D-Day" was to "V-Day" in World War II. Once the Allies had established a beach-head at Normandy on D-Day, victory over Hitler, the Nazis and the Axis powers, was virtually guaranteed. The remainder of the war subsequent to D-Day constituted the completion of a victory already secure and inevitable.

So it is with the resurrection of Jesus Christ from the dead. The great turning point in the history of redemption has been accomplished. We live in anticipation of the harvest which follows upon our Lord's resurrection. We live in anticipation of His coming again, when the almighty power of God in Christ, the power that overcame sin, destroyed death and defeated the devil, will be fully and finally revealed. We await the "revelation" of Him who by His death and resurrection has defeated all the powers that have been arrayed against us and has triumphed over them (Col. 2:15).

We live, therefore, in the end-time, when the gospel of the crucified, resurrected and ascended Lord is to be preached to the ends of the earth and disciples made of every nation. Meanwhile, as we anticipate His revelation from heaven, we live in terms of the confession that "Christ Jesus, who died — more than that, who was raised to life — is at the right hand of God and is also interceding for us. Who shall separate us from the love of Christ? Shall trouble or hardship or persecution or famine or nakedness or danger or sword? . . . No, in all these things we are more than conquerors through Him who loved us" (Romans 8:34-35,37).

Questions for Discussion

1. Read the four gospel accounts of Christ's resurrection (Matthew 28:1-15; Mark 16:1-13; Luke 24:1-12; John 20:1-18). What do these accounts have in common? What is distinctive to each account?

2. In 1 Corinthians 15:1-19, the apostle Paul provides an extensive defense of the reality of the resurrection. How does he demonstrate the reality of the resurrection? Is this a "proof" of the resurrection?

3. What is the saving significance of Christ's resurrection? What consequences follow, if Christ's resurrection is denied?

4. Identify common ways in which the resurrection of Christ is either denied or redefined today.

5. How does the resurrection of Christ relate to the believer's justification (compare Rom. 4:25)?

6. Why does the resurrection of Christ demonstrate that He was indeed the Son of God (compare Rom. 1:3,4)?

7. Evaluate the analogy used by Oscar Cullmann ("D-Day" and "V-Day") to relate the resurrection of Christ to the final victory of God at the close of this present age.

8. Why is it important to insist that the same flesh and blood body of our Lord that was put to death, was also raised on the third day?

CHAPTER EIGHT

"HE ASCENDED INTO HEAVEN, AND SITTETH AT THE RIGHT HAND OF GOD THE FATHER ALMIGHTY"

"And after He had said these things, He was lifted up while they were looking on, and a cloud received Him out of their sight." Acts 1:9

"And being found in appearance as a man, He humbled Himself by becoming obedient to the point of death, even death on a cross. Therefore also God highly exalted Him, and bestowed on him the name which is above every name." Philippians 2:8,9

Oftentimes we hear the complaint that people are, despite their apparent level of education and culture, rather illiterate. It is surprising, for example, to discover that in an advanced, industrialized and modern society like the United States, with its state supported and sponsored system of schools from the primary to the university level, there are many people who can barely read at a grade school level. I can still remember the discomfort I felt in asking a class of junior high vacation bible school students to take turns reading the Scriptures, when I discovered that some of them were unable to read. They were illiterate, though they had been students for many years!

Though the level of illiteracy is a serious problem in the society in which we live, it is a more serious problem for the church. For, in the church today, we often discover a different, and even more destructive, kind of illiteracy — people do not really know what the Bible teaches or the church confesses. This can easily he illustrated in terms of the article in the Creed before us, "He ascended into heaven, and sitteth at the right hand of God the Father Almighty." If there is any single article in the Creed which is little known or understood, it is this one. And yet this is one of the most important things that we can confess about our Lord Jesus Christ, especially in terms of His present work — that He is the ascended and glorified King who rules over all things for the sake of His church.

I can remember an occasion when a visitor to the congregation I served as a pastor in Ontario, California, inquired about the announcement in the bulletin concerning an Ascension Day service. Though this visitor indicated that she was a professing member of a Christian church, she had almost no knowledge or understanding of this article of the Creed. It had never really registered with her that, after our Lord's resurrection on the third day, He entered by way of His ascension into heaven and began with His session at the Father's right hand a new and decisive phase of His redeeming work in history. It appeared that her confession concerning the Lord focused upon a number of events in the distant past (He was crucified, dead, and buried, rose again on the third day) and an event still to come (He will come to judge the living and the dead). But her confession was only a blur when it came to His present circumstance and work! Sadly, this is true of many professing believers who are not literate about this important article in the Creed.

For this reason it is vitally important that we pause in our consideration of the Apostles' Creed at this article and ask what do we mean by the ascension of our Lord into heaven and His session at the Father's right hand? What does this tell us about our Lord Jesus Christ and His work of salvation? How does it benefit us to believe and confess this?

The ascension of Christ

The Apostles' Creed, when it confesses Christ's ascension into heaven after His resurrection from the dead, simply echoes the teaching of Scripture. Though the only full account of Christ's ascension is found in Acts 1:1-11, the New Testament frequently refers to or explicitly speaks of the event of Christ's return to heaven after His resurrection. For example, in the gospel accounts, we read that "He was taken up into heaven and He sat at the right hand of God" (Mark 16:19), and that "while He was blessing them, He left them and was taken up into heaven" (Luke 24:51). The apostle Paul says in 1 Timothy 3:16, "He who was revealed in the flesh ... was taken up in glory." Frequently, references to Christ's ascension speak of His returning to the Father who sent Him (John 7;34,36; 13;3; 14:28; 16:70-10) or of His present glory and power at the Father's right hand (Eph. 1:19-20; 1 Cor. 15:25,28).

The one full account of Christ's ascension in the book of Acts provides a simple, uncomplicated account of what occurred. Forty days after the event of Christ's resurrection, at the conclusion of His interim instruction to His disciples about the things concerning the Kingdom of God (Acts 1:3) and His promise of the future outpouring of the Spirit upon them, He was taken up into heaven in their presence.

> And after He had said these things, He was lifted up while they were looking on, and a cloud received Him out of their sight. And as they were gazing intently into the sky while He was departing, behold, two men in white clothing stood beside them; and they also said, "Men of Galilee, why do you stand looking into the sky? This Jesus, who has been taken up from you into heaven, will come in just the same way as you have watched Him go into heaven. (Acts 1:9-11)

It is remarkable how devoid the biblical record is of speculation and excessive curiosity about the precise nature of this event. Unfortunately, the simplicity of the biblical record of Christ's ascension has not been reflected in the history of the church's reflection upon this event. Though today the tendency among some is to ridicule or declare impossible the event of Christ's physical ascension into heaven, even in the period of the Reformation considerable differences existed between Lutheran and Reformed believers as to the meaning of this event. Among some Lutherans, the ascension was understood, not as a change in the *location* of Christ in His human nature from earth to heaven, but as a change of *condition* whereby His human nature passed into the full enjoyment and exercise of certain divine perfections, particularly omnipresence. This understanding of the ascension was associated with the view that Christ's human nature could be really present "in, with, and under" the outward elements of bread and wine in the sacrament of the Lord's Supper. For Christ in His human nature to be present in this way, it was thought necessary that His human nature become "ubiquitous" or able to be really present, not in any location only (namely, heaven), but in any number of locations at the same time.

Those who are acquainted with the confession of Christ's ascension in the Heidelberg Catechism, will recognize that this Lutheran view of the ascension is rejected in Lord's Day 18, when it says, "Christ is true man and true God. In His human nature Christ is not now on earth; but in his divinity, majesty, grace and Spirit He is not absent from us for a moment."[32] Following the Scriptures, the Catechism teaches that the same Lord Jesus Christ who was raised from the dead on the third day, has ascended in the genuineness of His human nature — that nature which He shares fully and completely with us — into heaven. The problem with the Lutheran understanding of the ascension is that it teaches that Christ's human nature was changed into something different and unlike ours (we cannot be, in our human nature, everywhere present!) in His ascension.

But why is this important? And how does it benefit us? Is it vital to insist that Christ ascended into the place called heaven in our human nature, a nature exactly like ours, though without sin

---

[32]*Ecumenical Creeds and Reformed Confessions*, p. 23.

and glorified through His resurrection from the dead? These are questions which naturally are pressing at this point.

When these questions are pressed, we need to recognize that there is a close and inseparable connection between the events of Christ's crucifixion, death and resurrection, and the event of His ascension. There are two aspects of Christ's saving work in particular that are tied to His ascension. These are: first, His work as our Advocate or priestly intercessor at the Father's right hand; and second, His work in preparing a place for us.

One of the themes frequently associated with Christ's presence before the Father in heaven is that of His advocacy or intercession on behalf of His people, those for whom and on whose behalf He offered Himself a sacrifice for sin (Rom. 8:34; 1 John 2;1). There are always two great tasks associated with the work of a priest in the Scriptures: the offering of a sacrifice for sin and intercessory prayer on behalf of those for whom the sacrifice was offered. In this work, the priest stands as a Mediator between a holy God and an unholy people whose sins require such an atoning sacrifice and intercession in order for them to have fellowship with God. Now it is precisely this which is so essential to Christ's ascension. As our only high priest He is able, on the basis of His perfect and complete, once-for-all sacrifice, to make a continual and effective intercession for us (compare, for example, Hebrews 7;21-28; 8:1-2; 9:23-28)! We may approach God and His throne of grace, because of the sacrifice Christ has offered and the priestly work of intercession which He conducts "for our interest" as our Advocate before the Father. By virtue of His ascension into heaven and the presence of the Father, Christ has entered into this new phase of His high-priestly work.

Furthermore, just as Christ Himself promised, His ascension into heaven and the presence of the Father means that we have been raised with Him and made to sit with Him in the Father's presence. As our Mediator, our Lord's ascension to the Father's right hand guarantees and pledges our place together with Him. Here again what belongs to Him as our Lord and Savior belongs also to us! This is also why it is so important to confess that by virtue of His ascension we have One who shares our nature completely in heaven! Perhaps one of the clearest and best known biblical expressions of this is the promise our Lord gave the disciples before His ascension in John 14:1-3:

> Let not your heart be troubled; you believe in God, believe also in Me. In My Father's house are many mansions; if it were not so, I would have told you; for I go to prepare a place for you. And if I go and prepare a place for you, I will come again, and receive you to Myself; that where I am, there you may be also.

This is the comfort which should be ours in the confession of our Lord's ascension. We now have a Mediator, One who intercedes for us before the Father's throne of grace. We have a Mediator, One who shares our flesh and blood and who is not ashamed to call us "brothers," who pleads our cause before the Father (compare Heb. 2:11). We have One whose advocacy is perfect and effective, since it is impossible that the Father would be unwilling to hear the advocacy of His Son whose sacrifice and intercession perfectly and completely satisfy for our sin. God has raised us up with Christ, and seated us with Him in the heavenly places, in order that "in the ages to come He might show the surpassing riches of His grace in kindness toward us in Christ Jesus" (Eph. 2:6-7)

The heavenly session of Christ

It is impossible, therefore, to speak of Christ's ascension and its benefits, without considering the consequence the ascension has for His present work as our Mediator. The ascension of Christ also marks the beginning of His "sitting" or heavenly session at the "right hand" of God the Father Almighty. It marks the beginning of a new stage of Christ's saving work. This saving work is not restricted to His high-priestly intercession on our behalf or preparation of a place for us in heaven with the Father. It also involves a new stage of Christ's saving work on the earth.

Notice that this article of the Creed for the first time speaks of Christ's saving work in the present tense — He sits at the Father's right hand. This is His present circumstance and this accounts for the kind of saving work in which He is presently engaged. In this respect, it is not exactly correct to speak of Christ's "earthly ministry" as though it were a thing of the distant past. Christ's "earthly ministry" continues today, but in a new and glorious way. Whereas He came to us in weakness, now He rules over the earth in power and glory at the Father's right hand.

This raises the important question of what we mean by speaking of His *sitting* at the Father's "right hand." In the Scriptures, the language of God's "right hand" is not to be taken literally but metaphorically (note that sometimes Christ is described as "being," "standing," or even "walking" in His present work at the Father's right hand; e.g.: Rom. 8:34; 1 Pet. 3:22; Acts 7:56; Rev. 2:1). The "right hand" of God designates a position and status of special honor and glory as well as of power and authority. Just as we even today speak of someone's "right hand" man, so we confess that Christ sits at the Father's right hand inasmuch as He participates in the Father's glory and acts on His behalf with the authority conferred upon Him.

This is why the Scriptures speak of Christ's sitting at the Father's right hand in terms which indicate that He has been granted the honor and privilege of exercising "all authority" and ruling over all things for the sake of His church and the coming of God's kingdom. In the so-called "Great Commission" in Matthew 28, this is expressed when Christ declares to the disciples, "All authority has been given to Me in heaven and on earth; go therefore and make disciples of all the nations ..." (v. 19). The apostle Paul also expresses this in emphatic terms, when he teaches that God has

> raised Him [Christ] from the dead, and seated Him at His right hand in the heavenly places, far above all rule and authority and power and dominion, and every name that is named, not only in this age, but also in the one to come. And He put all things in subjection under His feet, and gave Him as head over all things to the church, which is His body, the fullness of Him who fills all in all. (Eph. 1:20-23)

The Heidelberg Catechism proves once again to be an excellent summary of the teaching of God's Word at this point. In its summary of the meaning of Christ's session at the Father's right hand, the Catechism confesses that Christ is now the "head of His church" and the One through whom "the Father rules all things." From His exalted position Christ pours out His gifts, primarily His Spirit working through the Word, upon His church. He exercises His power and dominion on behalf of His church. Or, as the Catechism so nicely puts it, He "defends us and keeps us safe from all enemies" (Lord's Day 19).[33] In the fullness of that rightful authority which the Father has conferred upon Him in His heavenly session, Christ, our Savior and Lord, has been placed in charge of all things! "He must reign until He has put all His enemies under His feet" (1 Cor. 15:25).

Our confident obedience in the world

This confession of the ascension and heavenly session of our Lord Jesus Christ ought to be the foundation for our confident obedience as churches and as believers in the world. Just imagine it — we live in a world which is under the authority and in the care of our Lord Jesus Christ! The same Lord who was crucified in weakness now reigns in heaven at the Father's right hand. All of history is being moved forward and directed to its God-appointed goal by the Father's beloved Son, our Savior and Lord!

I use the word *confident*, because there is no other way to describe the posture of believers in the world when they live out of the truth of this confession. Though we may face difficulties of various kinds, though we may encounter powerful spiritual forces and movements ("principalities and powers") which array themselves against Christ and His chosen people, though we may discover even within the church of Jesus Christ evidences of apostasy and infidelity — we need not be afraid! We should not fear for a moment that Christ's cause or His church will be defeated. As Luther is said once to have observed, we do not tremble in our bed when we hear a leaf rustling in the wind even

---

[33]*Ecumenical Creeds and Reformed Confessions*, p. 25.

though it were the devil himself — for Christ is seated upon His throne!

But, I also emphasize that this produces a confident *obedience*. We must recognize that Christ reigns by His Word and Spirit, and that His authority is exercised primarily in the gathering, protecting and preserving of His church. This work involves the making of disciples of all the nations, "... teaching them all things whatsoever I have commanded you to do them" (Matt. 28:20). Christ works today, as the ascended and reigning King, in gathering disciples who are prepared to acknowledge Him as their Lord and Savior and live in complete and faithful obedience to His every commandment!

Our perspective here has to be that of Psalm 2. God the Father has decreed that He shall give to His Son, His Anointed whom He has installed as King at His right hand, the nations as His inheritance. Christ has been enthroned and His Word goes forth in power, calling all to faith and repentance. But as the reigning King, Christ does not issue His Word and Spirit in weakness or in the form of an "offer" that may be refused with impunity. He does not "invite" people to consider His claims upon them. He does not "suggest" that we will not find ourselves at odds with the world. Not at all! His Word which goes forth into all the world is a *royal summons*, commanding repentance (compare Acts 17:30) and calling to heartfelt allegiance to Him and His Kingdom. It is a royal Word, calling all to "kiss the Son, lest He become anger, and you perish in the way, for His wrath may soon be kindled. How blessed are all who take refuge in Him!" (Psalm 2:12).

Undoubtedly, there is much in our confession here that goes against the grain of popular piety and the practice of many who profess to be Christians in our time. This should not surprise us or make us lose hope. Our confession of the ascended, reigning Christ, a confession which often forms so small and unfamiliar a part of our faith, provides the only sure basis for continued and "confident obedience" in this world — until Christ comes again!

Questions for Discussion

1. Based upon your reading and study of the account of Christ's ascension in Acts 1:1-11 and other New Testament references, what was the nature of this event?

2. What is the biblical meaning of the language of Christ's being "seated" at the "right hand" of the Father in heaven? What other terms are used to describe His present position before the Father?

3. Summarize and evaluate the Lutheran understanding of Christ's ascension, especially its significance for what is called the "ubiquity" (everywhere presence) of Christ's body. Why is the debate regarding the nature of Christ's body (its local presence) in heaven an important one (compare the Heidelberg Catechism, Lord's Day 18)?

4. Identify and give the biblical basis for the benefits of Christ's presence before the Father in heaven.

5. Who is presently the "prince of this world," the devil or the ascended Lord Jesus Christ? Defend your answer from the Bible.

6. If Christ is presently reigning "until He has put all His enemies under His feet," how should that affect the present mission and work of Christian believers in the world?

7. Read Psalm 2 and describe the way it portrays the position and authority of God's Son. How does this relate to the "Great Commission" in Matthew 28:16-20?

CHAPTER NINE

"FROM THENCE HE SHALL COME TO JUDGE
THE LIVING AND THE DEAD"

"And they also said, 'Men of Galilee, why do you stand looking into the sky? This Jesus, who has been taken up from you into heaven, will come in just the same way as you have watched Him go into heaven.'" Acts 2:11

"For after all it is only just for God to repay with affliction those who afflict you, and to give relief to you who are afflicted and to us as well when the Lord Jesus shall be revealed from heaven with His mighty angels in flaming fire, dealing out retribution to those who do not know God and to those who do not obey the gospel of our Lord Jesus." 2 Thessalonians 1:6-8.

Most of us have probably heard or used some form of the cliche that "there is nothing more certain in life than death and taxes." Those who employ this expression do so to underscore the certainty, the inevitability, even the inescapability, of these two realities. Everything else in life is, by contrast, able to be escaped or avoided. But not so these two!

It is interesting, however, to observe that the Scriptures emphasize another certainty which we are often tempted to minimize or overlook. And that is the certainty of God's judgment upon our lives. Often the Word of God even links the certainty of death and of God's judgment closely together. In Hebrews

9:27-28 we read, "And inasmuch as it is appointed for men to die once and after this comes judgment, so Christ also, having been offered once to bear the sins of many, shall appear a second time for salvation without reference to sin, to those who eagerly await Him." Similarly, the apostle Paul writes in 2 Corinthians 5:10, in the context of describing the death of the believer, "For we must all appear before the judgment seat of Christ, that each one may be recompensed for his deeds in the body, according to what he has done, whether good or bad."

Perhaps the chief reason this certainty is neglected or minimized by many is that it suggests something foreboding and disquieting. After all — who wants to contemplate the prospect of standing before God's judgment seat, to be examined and judged according to what we have done in this life? How different this view of God is from the picture so many want to have of Him today! If God is conceived of as a kindly, gentle, almost "grandfatherly" figure who winks at sin and easily embraces the sinner, surely He will not be found in the business of subjecting His creatures at the final judgment to careful scrutiny or assessment. Surely He would not consign anyone, for example, to everlasting punishment — would He? It is not difficult, in other words, to determine why this is an aspect of our confession which is so often bypassed.

The Apostles' Creed, however, includes it in its description of Christ's person and work. Christ has been appointed to judge the living and the dead when He comes again. The last article and the only one to speak of the future work of Christ declares, "... from thence He shall come to judge the living and the dead." After Christ's ascension to heaven and at the conclusion of His session at the Father's right hand, He will come again to carry out God's judgment of all.

The certainty of Christ's coming again

The first thing to notice about this confession concerning our Lord is that it speaks of a certain future. All of the previous articles of the Apostles' Creed use either the past tense or the present tense to describe Christ's person and work. This article, however, speaks of the future. It speaks of something which the Christian believer expects or anticipates because it is promised in the Word of God.

This immediately underscores for us that Christ's present reign at the Father's right hand is one which is moving toward its God-appointed goal. The history of redemption under the present lordship of Jesus Christ, a history in which the Son is by His Spirit and Word gathering, defending and preserving His church, is moving unfailingly toward its consummation. Christ is coming! He is coming indeed!

The Christian believer lives, accordingly, out of the certain conviction that Christ who returned to the Father and sits at His right hand will come in the same way in which He went to the Father. In the New Testament, Christ's coming again is frequently emphasized and several terms are used to describe its nature. Sometimes it is referred to as His "coming" or His "being present" (compare Matthew 24:3,27,37,39; 1 Cor. 15:23; 1 Thess. 2:19; 3:13; 4:15; 5:23; 2 Thess. 2:1; James 5:7,8; 2 Pet. 1:7,13; 4:13); sometimes it is referred to as His "appearing" (compare 2 Thess. 2:8; 1 Tim. 6:14; Tit. 2:13); other times it is referred to as His "revelation" (compare 2 Thess. 2:1; James 5:7,8; 2 Pet. 3:4). Common to all of these references is the teaching that Christ will return visibly and bodily, and that His return will reveal or unveil for all to see the glory and power which are now His at the Father's right hand.

Unfortunately, this certainty and lively expectation of Christ's coming again has declined within the contemporary Christian church, particularly in the West. Sometimes this decline expresses an unbelieving denial of God's Word. Many "liberal" churches and theologians simply deny the biblical teaching that Christ will come again even as He ascended to heaven. Sometimes it is due to an excessive curiosity on the part of some Christians who try to determine the "time" of Christ's coming and the events which are thought to precede it. Who of us has not met someone who thought they knew the "day or the hour" of Christ's return? Because many of these attempts are fanciful and contrary to the biblical warnings against dating Christ's return, there has often been a failure to cultivate a keen awareness of Christ's return to judge the living and the dead. The Scriptural exhortation to be prepared for Christ's return has lost its edge for many. The inclusion of this article in the Creed, however, reminds us that this is an indispensable component of our confession of Jesus Christ as Lord and Savior.

The consummating act of Christ's exaltation

It should also be noted that this article emphasizes that the Christian expectation for the future focuses, not upon some general event or ill-defined final judgment but upon the return of Christ, the exalted Lord and Head of the church. Our hope as believers is that the same Lord who became incarnate, who suffered and died in our place, who was raised again on the third day and ascended to heaven, who sits at the Father's right hand — is the One who is coming again to execute God's judgment.

Thus, this article of the Creed echoes the biblical teaching that Christ's return is the consummating act of His heavenly session and exaltation. The coming again of our Lord marks the culmination and final step in His exaltation. He has been given, by virtue of His exaltation, not only the right to gather His church and exercise His authority over all things, but also to judge all men on behalf of the Father. The distinctive work of our Lord which is always associated with His return is this work of judgment.

In the Scriptures, this work of judgment is a special prerogative granted to Christ as Savior or Mediator. In the Gospel of John, Christ Himself is reported to have declared, "For not even the Father judges anyone, but He has given all judgment to the Son, even as they honor the Father" (John 5:22-23). The apostle Peter likewise describes the gospel the apostles were commissioned to preach as including this work of judgment on the part of the exalted Christ: "And He ordered us to preach to the people, and solemnly to testify that this is the One who has been appointed by God as Judge of the living and the dead" (Acts 10:42; compare Acts 17:31; Matt. 19:28; 25:31-34; Luke 3:17; Rom. 2:16; 14:9; 2 Cor. 5:10; 2 Tim. 4:1; James 5:9). Therefore, the Christian expectation is quite different from the general and often sub-Christian view that there will be a "final reckoning of sorts" or that all will undergo some kind of judgment by God in the end.

From the biblical descriptions of Christ's work of judgment, we can confidently confess that it will be a judgment of all men without exception, the living and the dead, believer and unbeliever alike. Moreover, all will be judged by the standard or measure of God's Word, particularly by what they have done with the gospel of Jesus Christ (John 5:22-27; 2 Thess. 1:5-10). Even those who have not heard the gospel preached will be justly judged and condemned by the standard of what God had revealed to them concerning Himself whether through the creation itself or by the witness of the conscience (Romans 1:18-2:16). This work of judgment will not be carried out in order to discover who will be saved or condemned. Rather, it will be carried out in order to reveal and to vindicate God's justice in the salvation of His people and the condemnation of the wicked and unbelieving.[34] It will be a work in which "God will judge the secrets of men through Christ Jesus" (Rom. 2:16) and provide a demonstration of the rightness of His final judgment or verdict upon the believer and unbeliever.

An encouragement for Christ's church

Because the Christian expectation of the final judgment focuses upon the return of Christ in glory and power to judge the living and the dead, it is an expectation which is deeply encouraging for Christ's church. The Christian confession of Christ's coming again is a key component of the gospel, the "good news" of our salvation through Christ. Even though for many the

---

[34]The biblical view of Christ's work of judgment leaves no place for what in Seventh Day Adventism is called Christ's "investigative judgment." In Seventh Day Adventism this work of judgment includes a "discovery" of who will be saved and condemned, and this discovery is based upon a doctrine of salvation according to works of obedience done in conformity to the law of God. Not only is this contrary to Scripture, but it is also incompatible with the biblical teaching that already in the "intermediate state," believers and unbelievers enter into a provisional and anticipatory enjoyment of salvation and condemnation. It is also fitting to note here that this biblical view of the finality of Christ's judgment is flatly contrary to any notion of a "reincarnation" or a second opportunity of salvation after death. We are all to be judged according to those works done while "in the body" (2 Cor. 5:10).

prospect of a final judgment generates fear and anxiety, for the Christian believer the confession of Christ's return to judge the living and the dead is a great comfort and joy!

In the passage from 2 Thessalonians 1 cited above, the apostle Paul reminds the church in Thessalonica of Christ's certain coming again (His "revelation from heaven") in order to encourage the believers in the midst of their present suffering and distress. Christ's "revelation" or coming will conclude their present pilgrimage as believers and bring to an end their suffering for the sake of the gospel, a suffering which included persecution by those who opposed the gospel and painful struggle with the remaining power of sin and darkness. Paul assures them that Christ's coming means that they will be granted the long-awaited Sabbath rest of God's people which the gospel promises. This is literally the word of encouragement in verse 7, where we read that God will "give relief to you who are afflicted and to us as well when the Lord Jesus shall be revealed from heaven with His mighty angels in flaming fire." Christ's revelation will bring rest and shalom to the people of God. It will mark the final step in Christ's exaltation, the completion of His saving work on His people's behalf. Consequently, the apostle adds strikingly that at His coming Christ will "be glorified in His saints" and "marveled at among all who have believed"!

This note of joy in anticipation of Christ, the bridegroom's, coming to receive the church, His bride, is a keynote in New Testament descriptions of Christ's return. Thus, Christ's return, far from being an occasion from which to shrink back in fear, is something for which the church prays — "Maranatha!" — and which she eagerly anticipates. For this coming will mark the beginning of the marriage feast of the Lamb and His bride (Rev. 19:7). It will mark the day of Christ's glorification in His people, in the completion of the work He has begun in them by His Spirit and Word. It is the day when the whole church will marvel at Christ when He is revealed. For this day will reveal the hitherto veiled glory and power of the bridegroom whom the church loved and for whom she eagerly waited (compare 1 Pet. 1:7-8).

The Heidelberg Catechism also underscores this joy when it describes the "comfort" of this article in the Creed concerning Christ's coming again:

> How does Christ's return "to judge the living and the dead" comfort you? In all my distress and persecution I turn my eyes to the heavens and confidently await as judge the very One who has already stood trial in my place before God and so has removed the whole curse from me. All his enemies and mine he will condemn to everlasting punishment: but me and all his chosen ones he will take along with him into the joy and the glory of heaven.[35] (Lord's Day 19)

As believers we may rejoice at the prospect of Christ's coming to judge the living and the dead, for we know and believe that the judge who comes has already been judged in our place. The judge who comes is also our Savior, Redeemer and Friend!

A frightening prospect for the unbelieving

Nevertheless, there is good reason that for many the thought of a final judgment, which concludes history and which issues in the fullness of salvation for some and the reality of eternal punishment for others, is frightening. This should not be surprising, since Christ's work of judgment will involve, to employ the language of the Catechism just cited, a condemnation of "all His enemies and mine to everlasting punishment."

Admittedly, this is not the kind of language commonly heard today, not even in the church! But it is the language of the church's confession which in turn echoes the language of the Scriptures. It is impossible to avoid, moreover, for invariably the Scriptures speak of Christ's coming again as a day of darkness and not light for the unbelieving and the impenitent. Furthermore, this is language which is found not only on the pages of the Old

---

[35]*Ecumenical Creeds and Reformed Confessions*, p. 25.

Testament. It is also found frequently on the pages of the New Testament.

For example, in the passage cited earlier from 2 Thessalonians 1, the Word of God uses strong and clear language to describe the fearful consequence of Christ's coming for the unbelieving, those who are enemies of Christ and of His church. Rather than paraphrasing this description, listen to what it says:

> For after all it is only just for God to repay with affliction those who afflict you, and to give relief to you who are afflicted and to us as well when the Lord Jesus shall be revealed from heaven with His mighty angels in flaming fire, dealing out retribution to those who do not know God and to those who do not obey the gospel of our Lord Jesus. And these will pay the penalty of eternal destruction, away from the presence of the Lord and from the glory of His power, when He comes to be glorified in His saints on that day, and to be marveled at among all who have believed. (vv. 6-10)

Similar language is frequently found in the Scriptures, so that the language of the Catechism is clearly consistent with the teaching of the written Word.

This demands our notice, not because this is a subject upon which the believer wishes perversely to dwell, but because it is a biblical emphasis notably lacking in contemporary preaching and teaching within the church. Various forms of "universalism" which endeavor to deny or minimize the reality of the condemnation of the unbelieving are increasingly popular, even among "evangelicals." The biblical teaching that Christ's coming will mean condemnation and eternal punishment for the unbelieving is often avoided like the plague, though it is an inescapable feature of the apostolic preaching of the gospel, To emphasize and teach, however, only half of the truth resident in this article of the Creed is not to preach the truth at all. Here, as is true elsewhere, a partial truth proves to be a falsehood.

This article in the Creed, therefore, presses home to each one of us the inescapable questions — do we practice as believers a lively expectation of Christ's coming again to judge the living and the dead? Does the prospect of His certain return evoke in us joyful anticipation or a fearful prospect of judgment? These are the questions, of course, of a preacher who has been called to preach the gospel. But I am a preacher, and these are the questions with which the gospel inescapably confronts us all!

Recommended reading:

Berkhof, Louis. *The Second Coming of Christ.* Grand Rapids, MI: Eerdmans, 1953.

Hoekema, Anthony. *The Bible and the Future.* Grand Rapids, MI: Eerdmans, 1979.

Questions for Discussion

1. Identify the different biblical terms that are used to describe Christ's coming again. What do each of these terms tell us about the significance and nature of Christ's return?

2. What evidence would you cite to show that believers and churches today have a lively or weak expectation of Christ's coming again?

3. What accounts for the fact that some "liberal" churches have almost no expectation of Christ's return?

4. In what way is Christ's coming to judge the living and the dead an expression of His present reign at the Father's right hand?

5. Summarize the biblical teaching regarding the final judgment (who will be judged? by what standard? for what purpose?).

6. Identify and evaluate the doctrine of Christ's "investigative judgment" in Seventh Day Adventism.

7. What significance might Christ's work of judgment have for our evaluation of the so-called "imprecatory" Psalms (the Psalms that plead for the Lord's judgment upon His and His people's enemies)? Consider 2 Thessalonians 1 in your answer.

8. What is "universalism," and how does this article of the Creed relate to this heresy?

CHAPTER TEN

"I BELIEVE IN THE HOLY SPIRIT"

"As for me, I [John, the Baptizer] baptize you with water for repentance, but He who is coming after me is mightier than I, and I am not fit to remove His sandals; He will baptize you with the Holy Spirit and fire." Matthew 3:11

"And when the day of Pentecost had come, they were all together in one place. And suddenly there came from heaven a noise like a violent, rushing wind, and it filled the whole house where they were sitting. ... And they were all filled with the Holy Spirit and began to speak with other tongues, as the Spirit was giving them utterance." Acts 2:1-2,4

One of the more controversial subjects within the Christian church today is that of the person and work of the Holy Spirit. Who is the Holy Spirit and how are we to understand His work? Because these questions receive a sometimes bewildering array of answers, there continues to be a great deal of confusion about the Christian confession of the person and work of the Spirit.

The most profound and influential expression of this confusion is the remarkable growth of the "Pentecostal" or "neo-Pentecostal" movements. One of the basic claims of these movements is that the biblical teaching concerning the person and work of the Holy Spirit has only recently come into its own in the church. Only recently has the church begun to experience the fullness of the

Spirit's power and gifts. This claim, together with the breath-taking growth of and diversity within the Pentecostal movement, has contributed to the uncertainty of many about the biblical teaching concerning the Holy Spirit.

Though this present confusion and uncertainty about the biblical teaching on the person and work of the Spirit demands more sustained attention, we will only consider the most basic features of the Bible's teaching concerning the Holy Spirit.

The Person of the Holy Spirit

In the sequence of affirmations which comprise the Apostles' Creed, the affirmation, "I believe in the Holy Spirit," is normally referred to as the "third article" of the Creed. It is termed the "third article" because in it the Christian church confesses her faith ("I believe") in the Holy Spirit as the third Person of the Trinity. This article reminds us again that the whole of the Christian faith focuses upon the Triune God, Father, Son and Holy Spirit, as the one, true and living God.

We must, accordingly, begin our treatment of this article by emphasizing that the Creed confesses the Holy Spirit to be one of the three Persons of the Trinity. Basic to the church's confession is her conviction that the Spirit is true and eternal God, co-equal with the Father and the Son. In this confession, there are two important claims, one concerning the *personhood*, the other the *deity* of the Spirit

It is important that we understand and stress the personhood of the Holy Spirit. Because of the vagueness which so often attends our conversation about and understanding of the Spirit, we can easily neglect to emphasize that the Spirit is one of the three Persons of the Trinity. We begin to think of the Spirit as an impersonal power, and not as a Person with whom we may and do have fellowship in the communion of the Father and the Son. This may even be betrayed by our speech, whenever we inadvertently refer to the Holy Spirit as "It" rather than "He." However, the Scriptures plainly teach that the Spirit is personal and we must discipline our speech to communicate clearly this truth.

There are several ways in which the Scriptures underscore the personhood of the Spirit. In the gospel of John, He is frequently designated the "Comforter" (John 14:16,25; 15:26; 16:7), the One who comes to be our helper and advocate. Only a Person answers to this designation and the role it reflects. For this reason, the masculine pronoun is often employed to refer to the Comforter (John 14:26; 15:26; 16:8,13,14).[36] Furthermore, when the Spirit's presence and work is described, the Spirit is said to hear, speak, witness, convince, glorify, lead, give help, and intercede for believers (compare John 14:26; 15:26; 16:7-15; Acts 2:4; 8:29; 13:2; 16:6; Rom. 8:14,16,26,27; Gal. 4:6; 5:17,18). The Spirit is One to whom we may lie or whom we may grieve (Acts 5:3,4; Eph. 4:30). None of these references can be understood, unless the personhood of the Spirit is presupposed.

Likewise, the Scriptures often testify to the deity of the Spirit. It is no accident, for example, that the Spirit is commonly termed the "holy" Spirit, for He shares in the holiness, the set-apartness, of God Himself. The Trinitarian name of God into which believers are baptized parallels the Holy Spirit with the Father and the Son (Matt. 28:19). When the redemptive work of God is summarily described, the Spirit is often included with the Father and the Son as the Author of our redemption (compare 1 Cor. 12:4-6; 2 Cor. 13:14; Eph. 1:3-13; 2:18; 3:14-19; 4:4-6; 2 Thess. 2:13,14; 1 Pet. 1:2). To lie against the Spirit is tantamount to lying against God (Acts 5:3,4). And to be indwelt by the Spirit is the same as being indwelt by God Himself (1 Cor. 3:16; Eph. 2). God Himself, in the person of His Holy Spirit, is present whenever and wherever the Spirit is present.

In connection with this confession of the personhood and deity of the Holy Spirit, one of the disputed issues in the history of the church has been the relationship between the Spirit and the Father and the Son.

---

[36]The use of the masculine pronoun is especially remarkable, since the New Testament word for the Spirit is a neuter noun. It is important to know these references in order to refute the position of the Jehovah's Witnessses and even some professing Christians that the Spirit is an impersonal power, not a person.

In the Nicene Creed, we confess that the Spirit "proceeds from the Father and the Son."[37] Though the Eastern Orthodox Church has never accepted this language, it expresses well the biblical teaching that the Spirit may never be isolated in His person or work from either the Father or the Son (compare John 15:26; 14:16; 16:7; 20:22; Acts 1:4, 8). The Holy Spirit works to bring us into fellowship with the Father *through* the Son. Indeed, the Holy Spirit's work is to glorify the Son and enable us to come to the Father through Him. This language of the "procession of the Spirit from the Father and the Son," therefore, provides a safeguard against any view of the Spirit which would allow for a fellowship with God the Father apart from the Son or find the Spirit present where the Son is neither known nor worshipped. The procession of the Spirit from the Father "and the Son" excludes any teaching that there is a general working of the Spirit apart from the Son from whom He also proceeds.

The work of the Holy Spirit

If the Holy Spirit is God Himself, one of the three Persons of the holy Trinity, what distinguishes His presence and work from that of the Father and the Son? Though all of the works of God are equally the works of the Father, the Son and the Holy Spirit, what work is "appropriate" to the Spirit?

In his monumental work on the Holy Spirit, Abraham Kuyper offers a useful distinction between the particular works of the Father, the Son and the Holy Spirit. He suggests that "in every work effected by Father, Son, and Holy Ghost in common, the power *to bring forth* proceeds from the Father; the power *to arrange* from the Son; the power *to perfect* from the Holy

---

[37]The Council of Toledo in 589 A.D. added the phrase, "and the Son," to the Nicene Creed, an addition which the Eastern Church rejected, leading to the schism between Eastern and Western churches in 1054 A.D. By rejecting the double procession of the Spirit from the Father "and the Son," the Eastern Orthodox Church opened itself up to a "mystical" theology which might permit a relationship with the Father apart from the Son.

Spirit."[38] According to Kuyper, we should think of the Father as the Author of all things, of the Son as the Mediator of all things, and of the Spirit as the Perfecter of all things. Whether in the work of creation or redemption, the peculiar work of the Spirit is the work of *perfecting* the will and purpose of God. The Spirit works *within* the creation and the creature to bring them to their appointed destiny or end.

Though this may appear to be too general a description of the Spirit's work, its usefulness will become more evident, if we consider, first and briefly, the work of the Spirit in creation, and second, the work of the Spirit in redemption (re-creation).

In creation

The work of the Spirit in creation is to perfect and bring to fruition the work of the Father and the Son. The Spirit actively molds and orders the creation, bestows and sustains the life of the creature, especially man, and directs the unfolding history of creation (compare Gen. 1:2; 2:7; Psalm 33:6; Job 26:13; 33:4). The "Creator Spirit" is the One through whom the world's foundations were laid and the life of the creature is upheld. Through His Spirit, God is powerfully active in a variety of ways to accomplish His will and purpose *within* the realm of His creation.[39]

In redemption

The work of the Spirit in redemption is to re-create, granting new life to fallen creatures who through the fall into sin are by nature dead in trespasses and sins. The Spirit is the One who

---

[38]Abraham Kuyper, *The Work of the Holy Spirit* (New York: Funk & Wagnalls, 1900), p. 19.

[39]It is interesting to observe that the biblical term for the "Spirit" in both the Old and New Testaments conveys the fundamental idea of "power in action." Jesus' description of the Spirit's working as like a powerful wind in John 3:8 (com pare Acts 2:2) nicely captures the point. Where the Spirit of God is present, like the blowing a mighty wind, God is present to effect his creative and redemptive purpose.

effectively and irresistibly applies to the elect all the benefits of salvation which are theirs in Christ. The fundamental work of the Spirit is to minister to us all that we have in Christ, completing *in us* all that Christ has done *for us* in His life, death, resurrection and ascension. Through the Spirit, we enter into the enjoyment of all the benefits of our salvation in Christ. The Spirit's work in redemption, therefore, consists in ministering to us on behalf of the Father and the Son all the gifts of God's grace.[40]

To make this more clear, there are several prominent Scriptural descriptions of the Spirit's work which deserve brief notice.

First, the New Testament describes the Spirit as the *One through whom Christ administers and applies His saving work.* Christ Himself continues to work in the gathering of His church through His life-giving Spirit (2 Cor. 3:17). For this reason, the great event of Pentecost in which the Spirit was poured out upon the New Testament church is a unique event in which the ascended Christ came in a special way to His people and continues subsequently to indwell and work among them (Matt. 3:11; Acts 2).

Second, the great work of the Spirit is *the work of regeneration* or the bestowal of new life upon people otherwise dead in trespasses and sins (Ezekiel 37; John 3:3; Rom. 8:10,11). The Spirit grants to us the new life which is ours in Christ. Thus, all the various aspects of our salvation — calling, conversion, faith, repentance, sanctification, perseverance — are so many fruits of the Spirit's life-giving work in us.

Third, the Spirit who ministers Christ's saving presence and grants new life is the *One who sanctifies us* (Titus 3:5; 2 Thess. 2:13; 1 Pet. 1:2). All those who are grafted into Christ by the Spirit and born again from above, are also purified and consecrated through the indwelling and purifying presence of the Spirit. They are by the Spirit in the process of being conformed to the image of Christ in purity, righteousness and holiness.

---

[40]There are several additional features of the Spirit's work in redemption which we can only mention here, but cannot consider: the giving of revelation through the inspiration of the Scriptures (2 Tim. 3:16); the illumination of the mind of the believer so that he can receive the testimony of the Spirit (1 Cor. 2:10-16); the anointing of our Lord Jesus Christ for the fulfillment of His office as prophet, priest and king (Matt. 3:16-17), etc.

Fourth, the Spirit is the *Spirit of adoption* (Rom. 8:15-17; Gal. 4:6) . Through the indwelling Spirit, believers are able to call God their "Father" and have the assurance that they are the children of God. And fifth, the Spirit is the *pledge of our full inheritance in Christ* (Eph. 1:14; 2 Cor. 5:5; compare 1 Cor. 3:21-23). The Spirit is the "downpayment" or "first installment" of the fullness of the inheritance which is ours in Christ. What we have now by the Spirit is a promise of what we shall have in full, when Christ's saving work by the Spirit is completed in us.

Conclusion

I began by noting the confusion which often reigns today about the person and work of the Holy Spirit. This confusion is often the result of a failure to focus upon the basic Scriptural teaching about the Spirit. This teaching, as we have seen, is that the Spirit is the third person of the Trinity, the One who *perfects* the works of the Father and the Son in creation and redemption. The work of the Spirit in redemption particularly is to communicate Christ with all his benefits to us, *to perfect in us* the work of salvation accomplished *for us* by Christ.

Consequently, the most important question we can ask about the Holy Spirit is the question whether the tell-tale marks of His presence and work are manifest in us. These marks are: union with Christ and participation in His benefits; the new birth which produces the fruits of conversion, faith and repentance; sanctification and renewal after Christ's image; the assurance of our adoption into the household of God; and a present enjoyment of an inheritance in Christ which will someday be fully ours.

In this biblical teaching concerning the person and work of the Spirit, we are again reminded that our salvation is all of grace, from first to last. Just as the Father is the Author and the Son the Mediator, so the Spirit is the Perfecter of our salvation. Indeed, only those who have been born of the Spirit can enter into the kingdom of God (John 3:5), for the Spirit alone perfects the Father's purpose and the Son's work in restoring us to fellowship with God.

Recommended reading:

Kuyper, Abraham. *The Work of the Holy Spirit.* New York: Funk & Wagnalls, 1900.

Packer, J.I. *Keep in Step with the Spirit.* Old Tappan, NJ: Fleming H. Revell, 1984.

Palmer, Edwin. *The Holy Spirit: His Person and Ministry.* Phillipsburg, NJ: Presbyterian & Reformed, 1974.

Owen, John. *The Holy Spirit: His Gifts and Power.* Banner of Truth Trust.

Questions for Discussion

1. Defend from the Scriptures that the Holy Spirit is truly God.

2. How would you defend the teaching that the Holy Spirit is one of the three "Persons" of the Trinity, especially against those who claim that the Spirit is simply a power or influence, not a person?

3. What is meant by the "procession" of the Holy Spirit from the Father "and the Son?" Describe the dispute about this between the Eastern and Western branches of the church. Why is this dispute significant?

4. How does Abraham Kuyper propose that we distinguish the unique working of the Father, Son and Holy Spirit?

5. What is the work of the Holy Spirit in creation?

6. What is the work of the Holy Spirit in re-creation or redemption?

7. In John 7:37-39, it is suggested that the Holy Spirit was "not yet" (before Pentecost). How was the Spirit present before

Pentecost and yet Pentecost is the decisive event of the Spirit's being poured out upon the church?

8. If the Holy Spirit is the "Author" of the believer's regeneration or "new birth" (John 3), how does the Holy Spirit work to produce it? Consider in your answer: 1 Peter 1:18-23; James 1:18; Canons of Dort III/IV.17.

9. Why is the Spirit sometimes called a "pledge" of our full inheritance in Christ?

CHAPTER ELEVEN

"I BELIEVE A HOLY CATHOLIC CHURCH, THE COMMUNION OF SAINTS"

"And I also say to you that you are Peter, and upon this rock I will build My church; and the gates of hades shall not overpower it. I will give you the keys of the kingdom of heaven; and whatever you shall bind on earth shall be bound in heaven, and whatever you shall loose on earth shall be loosed in heaven." Matthew 16:18-19

"To the church of God which is at Corinth, to those who have been sanctified in Christ Jesus, saints by calling, with all who in every place call upon the name of our Lord Jesus Christ, their Lord and ours." 1 Corinthians 1:2

Every so often we read newspaper reports summarizing the results of a poll taken on the subject of institutions in which people place their confidence. In these reports, we are given a ranking of institutions according to their standing and reputation among those polled. Frequently, among the institutions listed, the church is included. Sometimes the church ranks high on the list, enjoying a greater measure of confidence. Sometimes it ranks low on the list, suffering a decline in prestige and trust.

I mention this because the approach taken to the church in these opinion polls is radically different from the Christian confession of the church in the Apostles' Creed. In the approach of these polls, the church is treated on analogy with any other human organization or agency. The church is evaluated and judged as though it were little more than a social club, a political organization or a voluntary society of likeminded people. It is viewed without reference to God and His work in calling the church into existence.

However, in the Creed, the confession of the church finds its place only within the framework of the third article, "I believe *in* the Holy Spirit." The Christian believes *in* God — the Father, Son and Holy Spirit — and *therefore* believes a "holy, catholic church." This is not to say that Christians believe or place any confidence in the church as such. The church itself is never the object of our faith. Rather, the Triune God who calls the church into existence by His Word and Spirit is the One in whom we believe and place our trust. But no one can believe in the Triune God without confessing a holy, catholic church.

The "glory" of the church

Whenever we speak or think of the church of Jesus Christ, therefore, we must always remember that it is a community of those whom God is "calling out" of the world into fellowship with Himself. There would not be a church, a community of those who are gathered, protected and preserved by Jesus Christ, were it not for the gracious action of God. This constitutes the "glory" of the church.

The common terms for "church" in both the Old and New Testaments underscore this glory. These terms emphasize that the church is a community of "called out" ones, a "holy convocation" of those whom God has brought together, an "assembly" of those whom the Triune God has summoned apart.[41]

According to the Scriptures, God the Father, from before the foundation of the world, elected in Christ to save a people out of the fallen human race (compare Eph. 1:4ff.; 1 Pet. 2:9). The

---

[41]The two most common Old Testament words for the covenant community are *qahal* ("convocation") and *'edah* ("assembly"). The most common New Testament word, *ekklesia*, corresponds to *qahal* and simply means "called out." All of these terms emphasize that the church owes her origin and form to the action/s of God in calling her into existence. Thus, it is wrong to speak of "our" church. The church belongs to God!

origin of the church, accordingly, resides in the electing will of the Father. Furthermore, God the Son, in whom the Father elected to save His people and through whom, as the Word become flesh, their redemption was purchased, is gathering those whom the Father gives Him into His "flock" (compare John 10:25-31; 17:2ff.). The church is built by Christ as He gathers His "bride" to Himself (Eph. 5:32). And finally, God the Holy Spirit, whom the exalted Christ poured out upon the church at Pentecost (Acts 2), is the One who indwells and empowers the church, reaping the harvest from every tribe and tongue and nation (compare Matt. 3:16-17; John 3:5; Acts 1:8; 2 Thess. 2:13). The life and preservation of the church depends upon the power and presence of the indwelling Spirit. In short — the church depends for her origin, gathering and preservation wholly upon the divine initiative and sovereign grace of the Triune God.[42]

This means that, whenever we reflect upon the church or her existence in the world, we must always stand in awe of God's grace and mercy. The glory of the church is the glory of the Triune God's peculiar favor toward and gathering of His "chosen people" (1 Pet. 2:9).

"Mother of the faithful"

If the fundamental component of any Christian confession of the church is the conviction that the church is the fruit of God's

---

[42]The "holiness" of the church resides primarily in the "holiness" of God's redemptive acts in "setting apart" a people for himself. Consequently, all who belong to the church are "saints by calling" (1 Cor. 1:2), not only a select few, as in traditional Catholic teaching. Of course, the "holiness" of the church also includes the holiness of her members as they are sanctified by the Spirit. Though I will not devote special attention to the four "attributes" of the church (holiness, unity, catholicity, apostolicity) in this chapter, I would offer the following short definitions of the others. The *unity* of the church is the "spiritual [worked by the Spirit through the Word] unity in the true faith" which binds all true churches and believers together. The *catholicity* of the church is the "wholeness" or "fullness" of the church of all times and places, of the gospel, and of all Christ's treasures and gifts, in which all true churches and believers share. The *apostolicity* of the church designates the church's commitment to the apostolic "tradition," inscripturated in the New Testament canon, which constitutes the foundation of the church (Eph. 2:20; Matt. 16:18).

redemptive favor and work, then this has a further, important consequence — *only those who belong to the church have saving fellowship with God!*

Throughout the history of the church, this has been commonly expressed in two ways. On the one hand, the church has been called the "mother of the faithful" (*mater fidelium*). Speaking of this characterization of the church, Calvin once remarked in his *Institutes* that no one can claim to have God as his Father unless he has the church as his mother! Unless we have been gathered by the Word and Spirit into the fellowship of the church of Jesus Christ, we may not presume to call ourselves members of the household of God, children of the Father in heaven.

On the other hand, it has been confessed that "outside of the church there is no salvation" (*extra ecclesia nulla salus*).[43] No one ordinarily comes to be united with Christ and a partaker of His benefits unless they have been gathered into His church, where He is pleased to be present through His Word and Spirit. Thus, when in Psalm 87 the psalmist sings of the "glorious things" which will be spoken of Zion, chief among them is the joyful declaration, "This one and that one were born in her" (Psalm 87:5). The writer of Hebrews describes those who are saved as those who "have come to Mount Zion and to the city of the living God, the heavenly Jerusalem, ... to the general assembly and church of the first-born who are enrolled in heaven" (Heb. 12:22-23). The apostle Paul, speaking of those, both Jew and Gentile, who have been made living members of God's household, describes the church as a "holy temple in the Lord ... , a dwelling of God in the Spirit" (Eph. 2:21-22).

To our modern and secular ears, this kind of language, describing the church as the "mother of the faithful" and the exclusive community of those who are being saved, may sound radical and presumptuous. However, a careful reading of the book of Acts, or for that matter of the general biblical descrip-

---

[43]For example, the Belgic Confession, Article 28, reads in part: "We believe, since this holy congregation is an assembly of those who are saved, and outside of it there is no salvation, that no person of whatsoever state or condition he may be, ought to withdraw from it, content to be by himself; but that all men are in duty bound to join and unite themselves with it" (*Ecumenical Creeds and Reformed Confessions*, p. 77).

tions of the church, will show that the Lord Jesus Christ saves His people *by gathering them into the church*. Those who wish, therefore, to have fellowship with Christ, cannot dispense with His church!

The "means of grace"

To acknowledge that the church owes her existence to the work of the Triune God and that outside of her there is no salvation, raises the question of the concrete reality of the church. How is it that Christ gathers His flock into the fellowship of the church? What distinguishes the ministry of the church? Where is the church to be found?

In the Reformed tradition, the phrase "means of grace" has been used to answer this question. The church is to be found where Christ gathers His people *by means of the official preaching of the Word and administration of the sacraments*. These are the God-ordained media given to the church by which Christ through the Spirit communicates His saving benefits to believers.

Though there are a host of activities which may characterize the life of the local church, none of them can compare with these two. Indeed, the existence of the church depends upon the presence of the preaching of the Word and the administration of the sacraments. Without these means, there would not be a church. Only by them is the church able to prosper and grow.

In the so-called "Great Commission" of Matthew 28, it is interesting to observe that Christ singles out these means for special emphasis. The gathering of the church and the making of disciples occurs when believers are taught the Word of God and set apart through the sacrament of baptism. Similarly, in the account in Acts of the establishment and growth of the New Testament church, the church is called into existence through the preaching of the gospel and the administration of the sacrament (compare Acts 2:42; 6:7). Repeatedly in the New Testament epistles, the preaching of the Word of God is described as the fountain from which the church springs forth (Rom. 1:16; 10:17; 1 Cor. 1:21; 1 Pet. 1:23-25; 1 Thess. 2:13). Christ by His Spirit and Word is busy adding to the church those who are being saved, as they are brought to faith and repentance *through* the gospel (Acts 2:42).

The church is visible

At this juncture we do well to emphasize that these means of grace, by which Christ builds His church, belong to the "visible" church. Or, to put it more precisely, the church recognized in the Scriptures is always one which comes to visible expression in a particular place. When, for example, through the Word and Spirit, a people is gathered into the church in Corinth, there the church of Jesus Christ is to be found in all of its fullness. Accordingly, the apostle Paul writes "to the church of God which is at Corinth" (1 Cor. 1:2).

Though it has been traditional among Reformed believers to distinguish between the "invisible" and the "visible" church, this language unfortunately suggests that these are two churches. However true it may be that there are dimensions to the church which only the eye of faith can discern (including what I termed the "glory" of the church in the preceding!), the church is always a concrete, tangible reality. If you read through the Scriptures, you will discover that the language of 1 Cor. 1:2 is typical. The church of Jesus Christ is normally addressed in its concrete existence. It is the congregation of those who are "saints by calling" in a particular place. The church is to be found wherever there is a particular congregation in a specific location in which the means of grace are present.

It is vital to remember this, because it resolves some of the confusion that often exists today about where the church is to be found. Some people, for example, repeatedly make the mistake of simply identifying their denomination with the "church." But, strictly speaking, a denomination is not the church. It is a fellowship of "churches." As such, it is a manifestation of the church. However, the Scriptures ordinarily describe the church in its concrete existence as a community of those who have been gathered through the preaching of the Word. Wherever today we find such a church, in which the Word is purely preached, the sacrament properly administered, and discipline faithfully exercised

— there we may be sure that we find a true church of Jesus Christ, a full expression of the body of Christ.[44]

"The communion of the saints"

Though we can only consider briefly the phrase, "the communion of the saints," it must be emphasized that the church, whenever it is gathered by Christ through His Spirit and Word, is a living fellowship of believers. However important it may be to emphasize the primacy of the "means of grace," and thereby the official and organized character of the church's ministry, the church called into existence by the Word is always a *living organism*. The "holy, catholic church," as it is exists in any particular place, must be characterized by a fellowship between and among its members of mutual service and loving care.

Because believers who have been gathered into the fellowship of the church are joined in union with Christ, the head of the body, they are joined in the closest possible relationship as members of one body (compare 1 Corinthians 12-13; Romans 12). Because all members of the congregation are *in union* with Christ as members of His body, they are *in comm-union with* one another.

The Heidelberg Catechism well summarizes this aspect of the church, when it explains what we mean by our confession of the "communion of the saints": "First, that believers, all and every one, as members of Christ, are partakers of him and of all his treasures and gifts; second, that every one must know himself bound to

---

[44]Another way of making this point would be to say: were there only one local congregation of Jesus Christ on earth, we would still be able to confess, "I believe a holy, catholic church." This does not mean that churches of Jesus Christ ought not to enter into fellowship, denominationally or otherwise, to express their unity with each other. It only means that such fellowship is not absolutely essential to the existence of the church. Discerning readers will also detect in this sentence a reference to what are termed the "marks" of the true church. Though I am not considering these "marks" here, suffice it to say that these marks can only distinguish the "true" and the "false" church *where they apply*. And they apply, quite evidently, only to the church were the Word is preached, the sacraments administered, and discipline exercised, namely, the local congregation under the care of office-bearers who provide for the right use of the "means of grace." They can not be applied directly to a fellowship of churches or a denomination as a whole.

employ his gifts readily and cheerfully for the advantage and salvation of other members" (Lord's Day 21).[45]

Conclusion

One of the pressing needs within the churches today is a rediscovery of this biblical and Reformed understanding of the church. Many believers wrongly treat membership in the local congregation of Jesus Christ as merely a matter of personal preference or choice. Often you hear it said that a believer can have a "personal" relationship with Jesus Christ, whether or not they are living members of a true church of Christ! But this is an aberration, a distortion of the truth. Christ is pleased to gather a flock, a household, a communion. He is not gathering a collection of individuals.

Similarly, there are many who call themselves believers today who disdain and disregard the fellowship and mutual responsibilities that belong to membership in the church of Jesus Christ. They fail to acknowledge that the gifts and treasures they have received are to be used cheerfully for the advantage of other members. They are likewise unwilling to submit to the mutual admonition and discipline of the body of Christ! Some even make the serious mistake of treating a denomination or fellowship of churches as though it had a claim upon their allegiance superseding that of their ties to the church of which they are members!

All of this is contrary to a Scriptural view of the church. Perhaps one of the most important tasks facing the church at the end of the twentieth century, then, is the renewal of a doctrine and practice consistent with our confession, "I believe a holy, catholic church."

Recommended reading:

Kuiper, R. B. *The Glorious Body of Christ.* Grand Rapids, MI: Eerdmans, n.d.

---

[45]*Ecumenical Creeds and Reformed Confessions*, p. 27.

Zorn, Raymond O. *Church and Kingdom.* Philadelphia, PA: Presbyterian & Reformed, 1962.

Questions for Discussion

1. What difference does it make whether we confess to believe "in" or believe "a" holy catholic church?

2. What is meant by the "glory" or the splendor of the church?

3. Identify some of the common biblical terms and images for the church. What do they teach us about the nature and calling of the church?

4. What is the meaning of the expression, "outside the church there is no salvation?" How would you defend from the Bible this expression? Give examples of ways in which the truth of this expression is sometimes compromised.

5. Identify what is meant by the "means of grace."

6. In the Westminster Shorter Catechism, Question and Answer 88, prayer is also mentioned among the means of grace. Why would this Catechism include prayer as a means of grace? Do the official means of grace preclude the use of other means of communicating the gospel (personal witnessing, etc.)? Defend your answer.

7. Explain the distinction between the "visible" and the "invisible" church. What are the benefits as well as the dangers of this distinction?

8. How would you respond to the suggestion that the term "catholic" in the Creed be replaced by "universal," since the former term is liable to misunderstanding?

9. What does the phrase, "the communion of the saints," add to the believer's confession about the church?

10. If you were asked to choose between pure doctrine and warm fellowship in the church, how would you respond to this choice?

CHAPTER TWELVE

"THE FORGIVENESS OF SINS"

"The Lord is compassionate and gracious, slow to anger and abounding in lovingkindness. ... He has not dealt with us according to our sins, nor rewarded us according to our iniquities. For as high as the heavens are above the earth, so great is His lovingkindness toward those who fear Him. As far as the east is from the west, so far has He removed our transgressions from us." Psalm 103:8,10-12

It is often overlooked that the Apostles' Creed includes the article on "the forgiveness of sins" in the third part of the Creed. Our confession as believers of "the forgiveness of sins" comes within that part of the Creed which deals with the person and work of the Holy Spirit. Thus, we confess the "forgiveness of sins" within the context of the church and the communion of saints. This reminds us that it is only within the setting of the ministry and fellowship of the church that the Spirit convicts of sin, grants the assurance of pardon, and enables believers to forgive those who sin against them.

In considering this article of the Creed, accordingly, I would like to emphasize that this is the proper biblical context within which to confess "the forgiveness of sins." Only the Spirit working by the Word convicts us of our sin, our need to be forgiven (compare John 16:8). Only the Spirit working by the Word imparts the glad assurance and joy of the forgiveness of sins. And only the Spirit working by the Word brings us to the point where we practice the forgiveness of sins toward each other. In each of these respects, the forgiveness of sins belongs to the Christian confession of the church as the place of the Spirit's presence and working through the gospel.

Confessing our need to be forgiven

The first and most obvious aspect of this article of the Creed is its biblical assumption that we are sinners in need of God's forgiveness. Basic to the life and ministry of the church is this conviction that all men are sinners by nature and subject to the wrath and displeasure of God. This truth belongs to the heart of the gospel testimony which the church is called to make through her preaching of the Word of God to all the nations.

Though there have been some strange voices raised within the church in recent years, voices which have suggested that the gospel could be preached without calling people to a confession of their sin, the gospel is "good news" only to those who know and confess this truth.[46] The gospel makes no sense without the presupposition of man's sinful condition and its consequence in the way of alienation from God and liability to condemnation and eternal death. Indeed, the gospel would be an answer to a non-existent question, were we to deny the reality of sin and its consequence!

The Scriptures' testimony on the subject of sin is clear. From the account in Genesis 3 of the fall of our first parents, Adam and Eve, into sin and disobedience, to the extensive statement of the biblical teaching on original sin in Romans 5:12-21, the presupposition for the biblical history of redemption is the sad fact of man's sin. Whereas God created man for covenantal communion with himself — "after His own image, in true righteousness and holiness, that he might rightly know God his Creator, heartily love Him,

---

[46]Oddly, those who most vigorously argue that we not talk much, if at all, about sin, base their argument on the fear that such talk will "offend" people or scare them away. This is odd because the Scriptures themselves predict this "offense" of the gospel (1 Cor. 1:18ff.). It is doubly odd in that the gospel is designed to meet the need of sinners. Preaching the gospel without mentioning sin is a bit like proclaiming the cure for cancer, while not telling anyone that they have cancer!

and live with Him in eternal blessedness" (Heidelberg Catechism, Lord's Day 3)[47] — all have sinned and fallen short of God's glory (Rom. 3:23).

Consequently, in the opening chapters of Romans, the apostle Paul argues that all people, Jew and Gentile alike, are inexcusably guilty of worshipping the creature rather than the Creator and disobeying the law of God. As he summarizes the argument in chapter 3, "There is none righteous, not even one; there is no one who understands, there is none who seeks for God" (vv. 10-11). In chapter five of Romans, the apostle also insists that, by virtue of the sin of Adam, our first parent, we have all been constituted sinners, guilty and deserving of condemnation (compare Rom. 5:12-21). All men are by nature sinners, in a state of guilt before God and in a condition of sinful corruption. All are therefore subject to the reign of sin and death, liable to God's just condemnation and without any hope of redemption through their own good works.[48]

The Scriptures use various terms to describe sin. Sin is "missing the mark," missing the purpose for which we were created — "to glorify God and to enjoy Him forever" (Westminster Shorter Catechism, Q. & A. 1). Sin is "transgression" or "trespass," crossing over the boundaries of God's law and blessed order for human life in relationship to God and to neighbor. Sin is also "debt," the accumulated and unmet obligation which we incur each day afresh when we fail to love God wholeheartedly and our

---

[47]*Ecumenical Creeds and Reformed Confessions*, p. 9.

[48]It is important to remember here the distinction drawn between "original" and "actual" sin. We speak of "original" sin in order to refer to the sinful state and condition in which every human being is born. Original sin is "original" in two respects: first, all human sin originates with the sin and disobedience of Adam as our covenant head and representative; and second, all subsequent sin, the "actual" sins we commit, are the fruit and consequence of this original sin. By virtue of Adam's sin we are immediately and directly guilty before God. We are also born with a corrupted nature. Hence, we are guilty before God and liable to condemnation as participants in the sin of Adam not only, but also as those who personally sin as Adam's descendants.

neighbor as ourselves (Matt. 6:12).[49] Sin is disobedience and "lawlessness," the proud and faithless rebellion of the creature against his Creator (1 John 3:4).

What runs like a thread through all these biblical descriptions of sin is that *sin breaks covenant with God*. Sin is always described in relation to God. Our sin strikes at the heart of that blessed communion with the Triune God for which we were created. Sin is not "human error." Nor is it reducible to a "mistake" or "miscalculation." It is certainly not a "sickness" for which we are not culpable.[50] No, it is a fundamental and radical violation of the covenant relationship in which we were created. Sin is "offense" against God which alienates the sinner from Him and requires reconciliation and forgiveness.

Confessing God's provision for our need

Though this article of the Creed presupposes the fact of sin, it emphasizes *the forgiveness* of sins. In this article, we confess the heart of the gospel's message of good news, of salvation for all who embrace Christ by faith and accept the promises of God's Word. Lest we become guilty, then, of majoring in sin and minoring in grace, we need to move on to consider God's provision of forgiveness through the gospel!

If we seek a brief exposition of the forgiveness of sin, the Heidelberg Catechism helps us considerably. In reply to the question, "What do you believe concerning the forgiveness of sins?," the Catechism answers, "That God, for the sake of Christ's satisfaction, will no more remember my sins, neither my sinful

---

[49] It is interesting that our Lord taught us to pray, "forgive us our debts, as we forgive our debtors." Those who are children of God through faith in Jesus Christ are evidently guilty of accumulating new debts, new unmet obligations, each day, for which they need to pray regularly for forgiveness.

[50] It is instructive to observe how much our culture loves to employ the metaphor of sickness to refer to what the Scriptures term "sin." Sinful behavior is ascribed to some alleged sickness, whether physical or mental. Though the Bible does compare sin to sickness, it does not permit the use of this metaphor as a sufficient description of sin. The problem with this metaphor is that it removes the responsibility for sin from the one who sins. This the Bible never does.

nature, against which I have to struggle all my life long; but will graciously grant unto me the righteousness of Christ, that I may never come into condemnation" (Lord's Day 21).[51]

In this answer, the forgiveness of sins is based squarely upon Christ's atoning work on behalf of His people. God forgives the sins of His people "for the sake of Christ's satisfaction." That is, because Christ bore the punishment and curse due us on account of our sin, we "may never come into condemnation" (compare Rom. 4:25). God does not remember our sins *because* Christ Himself bore their penalty upon the cross. Moreover, Christ, by His life of perfect obedience, has fulfilled on our behalf all the obligations of God's covenant. By graciously granting or reckoning to us the righteousness of Christ, God forgives my sin *without abandoning His justice or minimizing the obligation of obedience* (compare Rom. 3:26; 5:17-19). Furthermore, this forgiveness through Christ God grants to those and those only who acknowledge their sin and embrace through faith the gospel promise.

That's why the setting for our confession of the forgiveness of sins in the Apostles' Creed is so important. Only where the gospel is being administered in the power and presence of the Spirit do we dare speak of the forgiveness of sins (compare John 20:21-23; Romans 10:6-10,13-21). Only where men and women are summoned through the gospel to "be reconciled to God" through Christ do they experience the forgiveness of sins (compare 2 Cor. 5:18-20). Only where believers acknowledge the *costliness* of Christ's "active" and "passive" obedience, His obedience on our behalf and death in our place, is there the forgiveness of sins. The forgiveness of sins is a *divine act* in which God is reconciled to us and we to Him through our Lord Jesus Christ. It is an act which requires a believing response. It is not a *presumption* which any careless and impenitent sinner may have before God!

Notice the striking contrast between this understanding of the forgiveness of sins and the way it is often misunderstood today. Most of us are probably acquainted with contemporary presentations of the gospel which are reducible to the slogan, "God loves you and so do I!" Or, we may be familiar with the phrase, "smile,

---

[51]*Ecumenical Creeds and Reformed Confessions*, p. 27.

God loves you," or the bumper sticker, "I'm not perfect, only forgiven!"

Though all of these slogans and phrases are frequently bandied about, even in Reformed circles, they at best dangerously mislead, and at worst militate against, the biblical teaching concerning forgiveness. They do so because they treat forgiveness as though it were cheap!

Those who deal in such slogans often neglect to mention that forgiveness was purchased at the price of Christ's satisfaction and perfect righteousness on our behalf. Not only is God presumed to be in the business of simply forgiving people for whatever sins they commit, but it is also presumed that He grants forgiveness to everyone — period! As a pastor's meditation in a local newspaper column I read recently put it, "[E]veryone should be happy all the time because God loves and forgives them!" This, he argued, ought to be the case for everyone, whether or not they confess and turn from their sin, or flee to Christ for mercy and grace!

The Christian confession of the forgiveness of sins, however, acknowledges that reconciliation and peace with God, including the forgiveness of sins, are granted only to those who embrace Christ through the gospel. Only those believers who can sing with the heart, as well as with the mouth, "Amazing grace, how sweet the sound, that saved a wretch like me," know what it is to confess the forgiveness of sins.

Confessing our readiness to be forgiving

Many students of the Bible are familiar with Jesus' parable about the "Unmerciful Servant" in Matthew 18:21-35. When asked by Peter, "Lord, how often shall my brother sin against me and I forgive him? Up to seven times?," Jesus responded by means of a parable which illustrated our obligation to be forgiving toward those who sin against us.

I mention this parable here, because no consideration of the forgiveness of sins in a Christian context is adequate, unless it also includes our responsibility to be forgiving. This is something which is repeatedly emphasized in the Scriptures (compare, for example, Matt. 6:12; Eph. 5:32).

Here too we have to be careful how we understand this mutual forgiveness. We are to forgive *even as* the Lord has forgiven us. This is a far cry from the tolerance of evil or acceptance of those who continue in unconfessed sin which some today mistake for forgiveness. For example, a husband who is unfaithful to his wife cannot say to her (nor should we), "You are obligated to forgive me" (him), when he is himself unwilling to confess his sin to the Lord and turn from it! Forgiveness always begins with confession of sin and reconciliation through Christ. Only within the context of the Spirit's work in convicting of sin and renewing the heart is place given to, and opportunity provided for, the forgiveness of our brother or sister.

However, when we are sinned against and our brother or sister acknowledges the sin, then we are obliged to forgive in turn (compare Matt. 5:23-24; 18:15). When we have been sinned against and the offending sinner acknowledges his sin, we *must* forgive and be reconciled to him. Or, to put it more accurately, we *may* and *will* forgive, *just as* we have been forgiven in Christ!

It is not that our readiness to forgive earns or merits God's forgiveness. Not at all. It is only that no one can be a recipient of God's gracious forgiveness in Christ — no one! — without standing ready to forgive. God never grants forgiveness without provoking us to be forgiving of others.

In that respect, the truest test of our confession of "the forgiveness of sins" is whether we *live by grace*. Those whom God has forgiven in Christ, who know that they live each day and are members of the church by grace alone, cannot but be forgiving of and gracious in their dealings with others.

Questions for Discussion

1. Define what is meant by "sin" in the Scriptures. Include in your answer and explanation some of the common biblical terms for "sin."

2. How would you respond to someone who says that, in the church of Jesus Christ, "we should only emphasize the positive and not turn people away by talking about sin"?

3. On what basis and in what way does God forgive our sins through Jesus Christ? What are the elements of true forgiveness and reconciliation?

4. What is the difference, if any, between "forgiving" and "forgetting" sins?

5. In the Lord's Prayer, we are taught as believers to pray, "forgive us our debts, *as we forgive our debtors?*" How does our readiness to forgive others relate to God's readiness to forgive us?

6. How should the Christian confession of the "forgiveness of sins" affect the way believers conduct themselves, especially in their dealings with others?

CHAPTER THIRTEEN

"THE RESURRECTION OF THE BODY, AND THE LIFE EVERLASTING"

"Therefore, being always of good courage, and knowing that while we are at home in the body we are absent from the Lord — for we walk by faith, not by sight — we are of good courage, I say, and prefer rather to be absent from the body and to be at home with the Lord." 2 Corinthians 5:6-8

"For our citizenship is in heaven, from which also we eagerly wait for a Savior, the Lord Jesus Christ; who will transform the body of our humble state into conformity with the body of His glory, by the exertion of the power that He has even to subject all things to Himself."Philippians 3:20-21

Comparing the old covenant believer with the new covenant believer, John Calvin remarks somewhere that both are called to live in hope. Even the believer who looks back in faith to the great redemptive events of Christ's birth, death, resurrection and ascension, must continue to look forward in hope to the consummation and completion of Christ's work in the future. As Calvin put it, the Christian always embraces Christ "clothed in His promises." Christian believers, by virtue of their union with Christ, await the day of their full and complete participation in the saving benefits of His death and resurrection. The whole course of the Christian's pilgrimage has, then, a forward look. It is dominated by the fact that we have been "born again to a living hope through the resurrection of Jesus Christ from the dead" (1 Peter 1:3).

I am reminded in this connection of a popular Christian song which includes the line, "I do not know what the future holds, but I know who holds the future." Though the intended meaning of this line may be clear and true enough — no one of us knows precisely what the future holds in the way of prosperity or adversity — it is not exactly accurate. We *do know* the main lines of the future *as it is in Christ.* Indeed, we have seen our future as believers in the past events of Christ's resurrection from the dead and ascension to the Father's right hand!

For this reason, the Apostles' Creed concludes with a twofold affirmation about the glorious future anticipated by the believer. We know what the future holds, at least in two, most important respects! The future which captivates and draws the believer forward is full of promise and rich with blessing, the promise and blessing of "the resurrection of the body and the life everlasting."

An entrance through death into Christ's presence

It is important to notice that the Apostles' Creed, when it speaks of the Christian's future, does not specifically mention the future of the believer who "falls asleep" in Jesus before His coming again and the resurrection of the dead. Because of the importance of this aspect of the believer's future hope and the confusion which often abounds today concerning it, we need to digress for a moment to consider this aspect of the believer's hope for the future, what is often termed the "intermediate state."

Interestingly, when the Heidelberg Catechism treats the Creed's affirmation of "the resurrection of the body," it begins by speaking of this intermediate state. In answer to the question, "What comfort does *the resurrection of the body* afford you?," the Catechism answers, "That not only my soul, after this life, shall be immediately taken up to Christ, its Head; but also that this my body, raised by the power of Christ, shall again be united with my soul, and made like unto the glorious body of Christ."[52] What is

---

[52]*Ecumenical Creeds and Reformed Confessions*, p. 28.

interesting about this confession is that it almost "*intrudes*" into the answer the subject of what becomes of the believer immediately upon death and the separation of body and soul which death brings.

I place the word "intrudes" in quotation marks because it is really not an intrusion at all. It is a necessary confession of faith and the expression of an important biblical teaching which is the source of great comfort to believers.

This biblical teaching is that the believer's *communion with Christ is not broken by death.* Believers who have been joined through faith with Christ and who are indwelt by the Spirit of God are, when they die, immediately taken into the presence of the Lord. The communion with Christ which they enjoy now is not interrupted, but rather intensified, upon the event of their death.

In 2 Corinthians 5, the apostle Paul describes this reality by comparing our being "at home in the body" to being "absent from the Lord" (v. 6). Conversely, he speaks of our "being absent from the body" as a being "at home with the Lord." When our present bodies are dissolved (v. 1), we will not be deprived of that communion with the Lord which we already enjoy in this life. Rather, we will enter into a new and more intimate communion in the Lord's presence.

Similarly, in Philippians 1, the apostle is able to speak of his death as "gain," precisely because it will bring him (and any believer) an even greater communion with Christ, his heavenly head! Writing from prison, Paul recognizes that he may well be put to death for the sake of the gospel. But he is not afraid because death would be better than life — "... for me to live is Christ, and to die is gain" (Phil. 1:21). Nonetheless, recognizing that the Lord may well have work for him to do yet on behalf of the Philippians and others, he adds, "... having the desire to depart and be with Christ, for this is very much better; yet to remain on in the flesh is more necessary for your sake" (vv. 23-24).

These passages and others (compare Luke 16:22; 23:43; Matt. 10:28; Rev. 22:4) clearly describe an unbroken communion of life between the believer and the Lord Jesus Christ, a communion which is not interrupted or suspended for a time upon the believer's death. Though we must guard ourselves here against any undisciplined speculation about the exact nature of this intermediate state of communion with the Lord, no one has the right to deprive the believing child of God of this comfort.

Consequently, we must reject several common ways in which this biblical truth and comfort have been and continue to be assailed. Some Christians prefer to speak of a "soul sleep" or an unconscious state which characterizes the period between the believer's death and resurrection. Due to an unwarranted fear of a so-called body-soul "dualism" or dichotomy, they deny any conscious fellowship between the believer and the Lord before the resurrection of the body.[53] In a somewhat similar vein, others suggest that believers are "annihilated" completely at death, in both body and soul, only to be resurrected subsequently at the last day. This view is largely founded upon the unbiblical assumption that man, who has been created a "living soul," cannot experience any continued existence apart from the body.[54] Finally, it is evident that the comfort of the biblical teaching concerning the intermediate state is lost in the traditional Roman Catholic teaching of "purgatory." There is simply no biblical warrant for the doctrine of purgatory, that believers will undergo after death a period (of greater or lesser duration) of suffering to finish their "satisfaction" of the temporal punishment of sin.

---

[53]This position is often due to an over-zealous interest in preserving against a supposed Greek distinction between the body and the soul. However, the Scriptures often distinguish between the body and soul, without depreciating the body or denying the psycho-somatic unity of man (compare Matt. 10:28; Heb. 12:22-24; Rev. 14:13); This view also misreads the biblical euphemism in which death is describes sometimes as a "falling asleep" (compare Matt. 27:52; 1 Cor. 15:6; 1 Thess. 4:13). The comparison in these texts is not between consciousness and unconsciousness, but between labor (including unrest and suffering) and rest or peace. For the Christian, death need not be feared because it is an entrance into rest and marks the end of our present suffering.

[54]This is a view frequently found among the cults and other groups, particularly the Jehovah's Witnesses and the Seventh-Day Adventists. But it would also seem to be the view most consistent with the insistence of some that the soul cannot exist apart from its relationship to the body. It is not only incompatible with the biblical teaching of the intermediate state, but also with the resurrection of the body, since it really amounts to the view that the believer will be *recreated* (from nothing!) at the time of the resurrection of the dead.

The glorification of our life through the resurrection of the body

Though Scripture promises the believer an unbroken and even intensified communion with the Lord during the intermediate state, this state remains a provisional and incomplete one. It is "intermediate" between the time of the believer's death and the great, eagerly awaited time of the glorification of the believer's life in Christ through the resurrection of the body. Consequently, the hope of every Christian beyond the grave is focussed ultimately upon his participation in the "harvest" which remains to be reaped now that Christ, "the firstfruits," has been raised from the dead (1 Cor. 15:20-23).

The Scriptural account of the creation of man teaches that he was created from the beginning a "living soul," a unity of soul and body fashioned for fellowship and communion with God (Gen. 2:7). Accordingly, there is not a hint anywhere in the Scriptures that man's bodily existence is a hindrance to fellowship with God. There is no suggestion of a dualism or dichotomy of body and soul, in which the body is denigrated. Man was created for life, covenant life with God, as a creature formed from the dust of the earth. His body was not in the beginning a "prison house" of the soul. It was the indispensable medium of man's creaturely life and his fulfillment of the mandate given him to have dominion over and provide a stewardly care of the creation.

But so it will be in the "world without end"! The biblical view of the believer's future promises the redemption of the whole man, body and soul, in fellowship with Christ. Redemption in Christ, therefore, includes the resurrection of the body.

There are several metaphors and images used in the Scriptures to describe the resurrection of the body and the difference between our present bodies, burdened and weighed down as they are by the consequence and curse of sin, and our anticipated resurrection bodies.

For example, in 2 Corinthians 5 the apostle Paul employs two metaphors to describe the resurrection of the body. On the one hand, he employs the metaphor of a dwelling place to compare the weakness and fragility of our present bodies with the strength and indestructibility of our resurrection bodies. Whereas our present bodies are like "tents" which quickly dissolve and pass away, our future dwelling will be like a "house, not made with human hands, eternal in the heavens" (v. 1). And on the other hand, he employs the metaphor of clothing to compare our present mortality and liability to death to our future immortality and immunity to death. Employing (mixing!) both metaphors at once, he declares, "For indeed while we are in this tent, we groan, being burdened, because we do not want to be unclothed, but to be clothed, in order that what is mortal may be swallowed up by life" (v. 4).

In Philippians 3, the apostle describes the believer as someone whose citizenship is "in heaven" and who eagerly awaits for the Savior to come from there. For, when the Savior is revealed, He "will transform the body of our humble state [lit. "the body of our humiliation"] into conformity with the body of His glory, by the exertion of the power that He has even to subject all things to Himself" (v. 21). The language of this text promises us that one of the great acts of Christ's present reign at the Father's right hand will be this work of granting to the believer a full share in the power of His resurrection. Christ's glory as the risen Lord, as One in whom the power of sin and death has been vanquished, will be shared with all believers who receive bodies like His.

Furthermore, in 1 Corinthians 15, the relation between the believer's present, perishable body and his future, imperishable body is described under the figure of a "seed" which is sown in one form, but which, after it dies, gives birth to a new and significantly different form of life. Thus, the apostle writes, "So also is the resurrection of the dead. It is sown a perishable body, it is raised an imperishable body; it is sown in dishonor, it is raised in glory; it is sown in weakness, it is raised in power; it is sown a natural body, it is raised a spiritual body" (vv. 42-44).

Although these passages do not answer all our curious questions about the nature of this resurrection body, they clearly teach that *our present bodies will undergo a transformation, a transfiguration,* such that this mortal will put on immortality, this corruptible, incorruption. There will be a measure of real continuity between our present and our resurrection bodies. This body will be transformed and glorified.[55] And there will also be a measure of real discontinuity between our present and our resurrection bodies. This body will be changed, resurrected in the "twinkling of an eye," so that all will have become new.

The blessedness of everlasting life on the new earth

It is only fitting that this confession of the resurrection of the body should be followed by the confession of "the life everlasting." Those who share in the victory won for them by Christ over sin and death, who are raised incorruptible, anticipate the blessedness of everlasting life on the new earth. Believers eagerly await the fullness and completion of that new life which is already theirs now in the power and presence of the Holy Spirit.

The key word in this affirmation of "the life everlasting" is the word "life." The believer's future is one in which that *life in covenant communion* with the Triune God for which man was created will be realized in all the elect, the new humanity. "Paradise lost" will become "paradise regained."

The Heidelberg Catechism, in its summary of the biblical teaching concerning the "life everlasting," rightly calls to our attention how limited is our understanding of this blessedness of everlasting life on the new earth. To the question, "What comfort do you derive from the article of *the life everlasting*?," it replies, "That, since I now feel in my heart the beginning of eternal joy, after this life I shall possess perfect bliss, such as eye has not seen nor ear heard, neither has entered into the heart of man — therein to praise God forever" (Lord's Day 22).[56]

---

[55]There is presently a dispute which has created quite a stir in North American evangelical circles concerning the degree of continuity between this resurrection body and our present body. The chief figures in the dispute are the well-known author Norman Geisler and Murray J. Harris, who teaches at Trinity Evangelical Divinity School. See: Norman Geisler, *The Battle for the Resurrection* (Nashville, TN: Thomas Nelson, 1989); and Murray J. Harris, *From Grave to Glory* (Grand Rapids, MI: Zondervan, 1990). Geisler has accused Harris of denying the continuity between our present and resurrection bodies, and suggested that Harris' ministerial status be taken away by the Evangelical Free Church of America.

[56]*Ecumenical Creeds and Reformed Confessions*, p. 28.

Though we can only speak within the boundaries of what the Scripture reveals about this life everlasting, perhaps the best approach is to remember that this life will be the fulfillment and perfection of the new life in the Spirit we have already begun to taste in this life. Speaking of the believer's future state and the resurrection of the body, the apostle Paul states that "He who has prepared us for this very purpose is God, who gave to us the Spirit as a pledge" (2 Cor. 5:5). The term used here to describe the Spirit ("pledge") refers to a downpayment which guarantees the full payment yet to come. Furthermore, it is a downpayment *in kind*, that is, of a piece with what will be given in full in the future. Thus, the apostle supports the idea that "the beginning of eternal joy" which the believer is given already now by the Spirit, is of a piece with that fullness of joy without end that awaits him!

As believers we know the beginning of this joy — the forgiveness of sins, adoption through Christ into the household of God, reconciliation and peace with God, the sanctifying presence and work of the Spirit, preservation through perseverance in the midst of trials, and the promise of the resurrection of the body and the life everlasting. Someday, in the life everlasting, we will know this joy in fullness and perfection.

And so we return to the point where we began. These words of the Creed — "I believe ... the resurrection of the body and the life everlasting" — remind us that believers embrace Christ "clothed in His promises." The future promised in the gospel is the future of Christ. The resurrection of the body and the life everlasting are promised to all who through faith share in all His benefits.

How fitting that the Apostles' Creed should end its summary of the Christian faith where the book of Revelation ends — "He who testifies to these things says, 'Yes, I am coming quickly.' Amen. Come, Lord Jesus. The grace of the Lord Jesus be with all. Amen" (Rev. 22:20-21).

Recommended Reading:

Schilder, Klaas. *Heaven — What Is It?* Grand Rapids, MI: Eerdmans, 1950.

William Hendriksen, *The Bible on the Life Hereafter.* Grand
Rapids: Baker Book House, 1963.

Questions for Discussion

1. What is meant by the expression, "the intermediate state"?
   How would you describe the state of the believer between
   death and resurrection at the last day?

2. Some people speak of a "soul sleep" to describe the intermediate state. In the light of the Bible's teaching, evaluate the
   legitimacy of this language to describe the intermediate state.

3. Define and evaluate the Jehovah's Witness and Seventh Day
   Adventist view of the relation between body and soul.

4. Why is the biblical doctrine of the resurrection of the body
   such an important and integral part of the Christian's hope for
   the future?

5. What biblical evidence would you cite to show that the
   resurrection body will be similar, though different in some
   ways, from our present bodies?

6. In the light of the Christian confession of the resurrection,
   how should the bodies of those who are deceased be treated?
   In this connection, evaluate the practice of cremation.

7. What does the Christian confession of a "new heaven *and
   earth*" tell us about the final state of glory in God's eternal and
   consummate kingdom? How concretely and realistically should
   we take the biblical descriptions of the final state?